BICYCLE TOURING

How to Prepare for Long Rides

Steve Butterman

WILDERNESS PRESS

Design by Kathy Morey and Thomas Winnett
Cover design by Larry Van Dyke
Cover photo © 1994 Michael Lanza

Library of Congress Card Number 94-26226
International Standard Book Number 0-89997-174-1

Printed in the United States of America
Published by **Wilderness Press**
          2440 Bancroft Way
          Berkeley, CA 94704
          (510) 843-8080

          Write or call for free catalog

Library of Congress Cataloging-in-Publication Data

Butterman, Steve.
    Bicycle touring : how to prepare for long rides / by Steve Butterman.
        p. cm.
    Includes index.
    ISBN 0-89997-174-1
    1. Bicycle touring. 2. Bicycle touring—Equipment and supplies.
    I. Title.
    GV1044.B88 1994   94-26226
                                     CIP

With love,
for my Mother

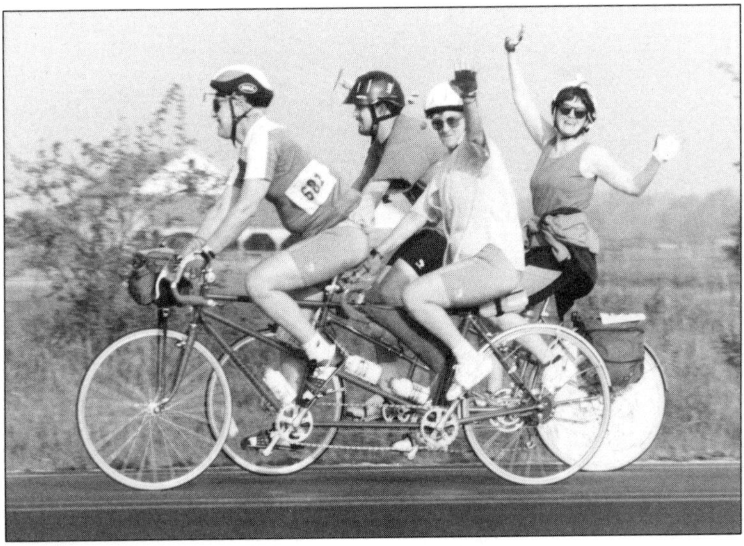

TOSRV photo by Greg Siple

Acknowledgments

I gratefully acknowledge the contributions of the following: Brenda Dunford, Greg Haldeman, and Earl Musick, for artistic contributions; Toby Pyle and Greg Siple, for photographs; my parents, Greg "BluesHowler" Striker, and Bill and Tammy Butterman, for working space; Kathy and the staff at the Bucyrus Public Library, for hunting down requested books; Ed Miller and Rocky Rhoades, for technical input and loaned equipment; Thomas Winnett, for editorial patience and guidance; Beth Thomas and John Wanamaker, for sharing dreams and visions; Angel Fausnaugh and Lori Striker, for support, friendship, and laughter.

——Steve Butterman

Contents

Contents

Introduction

There is more to life than increasing its speed.
——Mohandas K. Ghandi

Now I see the secret of the making of the best persons,
It is to grow in the open air and to eat and sleep with the earth.
——Walt Whitman

This book is designed to help you plan, prepare for, and visualize a long-distance bike tour. Traveling by bike is an extremely rewarding, potentially life-altering experience; proper planning and preparation help to make it so.

If you are concerned about whether you actually can complete a long bike tour, I assure you: *Yes, you can.* Not your age, not your financial circumstances, not even your current fitness level or cycling experience matters much right now. What does matter is your *desire*; if you have a strong desire to explore your country or your world by bicycle, you can.

You will first need to equip yourself well, but that does not necessarily mean expensively. Money-saving tips abound in Chapter 1, "Oh, the Things You'll Need." This chapter addresses equipment selections, from bicycles to odds and ends. After equipment options, I'll discuss loading your bike with equipment, and then riding it.

Chapter 2's topic is "Armchair Travel." You can extract much anticipatory pleasure from planning and envisioning a tour. To help you, this chapter includes sections on helpful organizations, map sources and mapping technique, research sources and strategies, and reading. That last section reviews and recommends splendid road narratives written by those who have toured vast distances by bike. Reading these books, you'll find that the cyclist-authors were not superwomen and supermen but thoroughly human—all the more so because of their cycling adventures.

Chapter 3 examines, in a question-answer format, "The Road Ahead." Here, I anticipate your most likely pre-tour concerns about on-tour situations and potential problems. As you'll see, with preparation, creativity, and good humor, no problems prove unsolvable, no obstacles insurmountable.

While considering roads ahead, you'll wonder where those roads might someday lead you. Possibilities throughout our round, fertile planet are discussed in Chapter 4, "Where You Might Wander." Few limits exist regarding the places you can ride to and through. Of course, it is not within the scope of this *Short Guide* to detail itineraries throughout the world; instead, I summarize general relevant conditions for each world region and identify additional sources of specific information—books, cycling clubs, organizations, and government sources.

The Appendices include an equipment checklist; selected mail-order sources of equipment, books, and maps; and tourist bureaus for all of North America and selected countries worldwide. Watch for time-saving, money-saving toll-free numbers in bold print in the appendices and elsewhere in the book.

The bike-touring facts and strategies are presented succinctly, in non-technical terms. In addition to the essentials that concern *all* touring cyclists, special attention is given to the special concerns of cost-conscious, international, and women bike tourists. I also refer you to many additional resources, including dozens of books. If your local library does not have a title, ask about their "Inter-library exchange" program, whereby you can access books from libraries throughout your region. Other relevant book sources are identified in the text and Appendices 3 and 4.

Be your tour next month or next year, down the road or round-the-world, you have ahead of you a journey of inner and outer discovery. I sincerely hope that you take that journey, and that this book helps you along. ᚛

Chapter One:
Oh, the Things You'll Need

A linen shirt, for example, is, strictly speaking, not a necessary of life.
——Adam Smith

*If I have got to drag my trap, I will take care that it be a light one
and do not nip me in a vital part.*
——Thoreau

This chapter discusses the things you'll need for your tour. (All equipment items discussed are also listed in Appendix 1, an equipment checklist.) Although some cyclists "tour" from motel to motel with not much more than their bike, credit cards, and a change of clothes, the typical bike tourist—a true adventurer and rugged individualist like you and me—spends most nights outdoors. Called "self-contained" touring, this is indisputably the most satisfying style of touring. It does, however, require carrying nearly everything you might need.

To be able to manage a variety of circumstances, you must equip yourself well. Incur a cut? Pull out a bandage! Get a flat tire? Pull out your patch kit and pump! Need to stop for the night? Get out your ultralight camping gear!

It is likewise important to minimize equipment bulk and, especially, weight. Every ounce must be pedaled up every steep hill and into every stiff headwind. Also, the bulkier your load, the greater your wind resistance. In selecting equipment, prefer the small, the light, the simply functional.

Throughout this chapter, I'll show you how to minimize weight and bulk without sacrificing your touring comfort and pleasure. One concept that will occasionally appear is "double duty": when a piece of equipment serves two functions—say, a detachable bike light that can also serve as a camp flashlight—this is called double duty. Search out such items!

When selecting equipment, you need to know which items are essential and which are not. To guide you, I have labeled items as either "Essential" or "Optional." Although some optional items are highly recommended, none are essential; if you have them or the means to get them, fine; however, you will do well to exercise restraint, taking only those optional items that come closest to fitting your personal needs.

The type of tour that you take will influence your equipment choices. Generally, the longer the tour, especially through distant lands, the longer your equipment list. The type of planned overnight accommodations further affects your choices; more nights spent outdoors means more equipment. Finally, expected climatic conditions will affect your choices, especially excessive rainfall and uncomfortable temperatures. Another factor is your budget. If money is no object, buy top quality in all categories, but don't take much more than you need. If money *is* an object, optional items can be skipped and essential items can be had at a bargain. This chapter has substantial cost-cutting advice for the cost-conscious adventurer. With creativity and determination, not only can you undertake and complete a long bike tour, but you can do so surprisingly cheaply.

The most important "equipment" is not for sale, but is within yourself: your big heart, your open mind, your persistence, your adaptability, and, especially, your sense of humor. Without these, the finest material equipment lies useless; with these, the scantiest material equipment shines and performs.

Have fun accumulating equipment. Shop around. Obtain a few items here, a few items there. If your tour is yet many months away, use a box or a laundry basket or a corner of your room for a "morale booster pile" of small equipment items. Watch it grow as departure day nears.

This chapter's main sections are The Bike, Attachments, Bags, Camping Gear, Kits, Clothing, Odds and Ends, Loading the Bike, and Riding the Loaded Bike. First, let's examine that most essential piece of equipment . . .

The Bike

Right off, know that *nearly any mechanically sound bike that fits you will suffice.* A century ago, cyclists crossed continents on one-speed bikes, some of them brake-less. On my last long tour, my fine built-for-touring bike was stolen in Las Vegas. Low on cash, I purchased a heavy old Schwinn 10-speed at a swap meet for 30 bucks. Straining at times, I made it on that old bike, trouble-free, over the approximately 300 rugged mountainous miles between Vegas and Southern California. I've met long-distance adventurers on similarly unsophisticated bikes, others on costly sophisticated bikes, others on mountain bikes, others on tandems (and on foot, on horseback, on skateboard). If you're compelled to go, the style and brand of the vehicle are secondary.

Built-for-Touring Bikes

A quality built-for-touring bike is worth its price if you can and care to spend the money. Unlike bikes built for speed, a new top-quality touring bike can be had for under $500, sometimes well under $400, especially if you find a used one in good repair or last year's model. Most major bike manufacturers make at least one version of the built-for-touring bike, and all but the smallest bike shops sell them. You can obtain detailed information about specific models through cycling-magazine articles, bike- shop personnel, mail-order equipment dealers, or correspondence with manufacturers. Consulting a trusty bike-shop manager or mechanic is simplest.

If Trek or Schwinn is all that your local bike shop carries, both manufacturers offer several styles of reasonably priced, quality touring bikes. I have toured on Schwinn touring bikes for thousands of miles with no problems and great satisfaction.

The main advantages of built-for-touring bikes include durability, riding comfort, suitable gear ratios, and relatively low weight (typically between 25 and 30 pounds). These advantages are standard on good touring bikes.

A touring bike's frame is strong, durable, relatively light, and designed for riding comfort. For lightweight strength and durability, the frame tubing is brazed, not welded, at the joints, and the double-butted (twice as thick at the joints) frame material is usually high-tensile alloy. Aluminum poses a breakage risk on a loaded touring bike. Titanium is sufficiently strong and exceptionally light, but very expensive. For comfort, the frame is semirigid, with wide angles at the joints, and with space between the wheels and the down tube and seat tube (see Figure 1); that way, the bike absorbs road shocks and distributes them throughout the stretched frame. By contrast, "fast" bikes' frames are rigid and pulled-in, with severe angles at the joints and less of a slant to the tubing and the forks. But you're going on a tour, not a race, and all-day comfort is priceless.

Quality touring bikes also feature low gearing. This is an extremely important feature for loaded bike riding, especially up hills. The low gearing is typically made possible with a very small front chain-ring called either a "granny gear" or an "alpine gear." Depending on whether the rear gear-cluster has 5, 6, or 7 cogs, this results in a 15, 18, or 21 speed. Fifteen speeds, the norm on touring bikes, is sufficient. With a 15

FIGURE 1

- ❶ rear derailleur
- ❷ freewheel
- ❸ seat stay
- ❹ chain stay
- ❺ seat tube
- ❻ front derailleur
- ❼ chainwheel
- ❽ top tube
- ❾ down tube
- ❿ handlebar gooseneck

A granny gear is the smallest chain ring

speed, you can conquer mountain roads. If you already own a dearly beloved 10 or 12 speed that you'd like to tour on, you could add a small third chain-ring, but this procedure usually requires a new rear derailleur and other costly modifications—consult a bike mechanic.

Other standard features of quality touring bikes include cantilever brakes, easy adaptation to attachments, and an appropriate wheel design. Cantilever brakes, standard on mountain and cross bikes, too, exert strong pressure over several inches of rim, capably stopping a rolling loaded bike. Touring bikes also have eyelets for simple, direct attachment of your racks and water bottle cages. As to wheel design, aluminum-alloy wheels are ideal, sized for relatively wide tires like 1¼"; the wheels should have relatively thick spokes—14-gauge spokes work well—and a few extra spokes (40 total) on the rear wheel. Most new American bikes, like most European bikes, now come with 700cm rather than 27" wheels. As I write, 27" tires are still the most widely available, and you may have difficulties finding replacement 700cm tires outside of American cities and European countries where these are the norm. If replacement tires will be scarce where you'll tour, take one and arrange for the folks back home to periodically send you additional ones.

Fit, and Component Positioning

The proper fit of any bike to your body allows riding efficiency and comfort. Just as surely as a hiker must avoid ill-fitting shoes, a cyclist must avoid an ill-fitting bike. When standing flat-footed over the crossbar, your crotch should clear it by an inch or so. When sitting on the saddle and pedaling, your knees should be almost—not quite—fully extended on the downstroke. Too small a frame will cause pedaling inefficiency and discomfort; worse yet, too large a frame will cause you to weave back and forth with your pedaling motion; such weaving is uncomfortable, inefficient, and a source of crotch-area chafing due to movement on the saddle. Ride a bike that fits!

Close attention to the adjustable positioning of certain bike components pays off. You can adjust your saddle up or down for while-pedaling fit as discussed above, so long as you do not adjust it too high (your seat post will have a mark indicating maximum height adjustment). Keep your saddle either level or tilted slightly down at the nose, but never tilted upward. The standard "drop" handlebars (see Figure 1) allow multiple hand positions—recommended for all-day riding. You can adjust your handlebar height, preferably an inch or so lower than the saddle; avoid adjusting it higher than the saddle.

When sitting on the saddle with your hands atop the handlebars, a 45-degree angle of your back is ideal for comfort, for handling, and for minimizing wind resistance.

If your torso is proportionately longer than your legs, a bike that fits you height-wise (top priority) may seem too small lengthwise; in that case, obtain a longer handlebar-gooseneck that will allow you the ideal 45-degree angle.

Through strategic positioning of your shifters and brake levers, you further increase your riding comfort and efficiency. Place your brake levers just above the curve on drop handlebars. That way, you'll be sufficiently low for stability when braking, and you can loop your thumbs around the brake-lever hoods for an additional riding position. Standard shifter positioning is on the downtube, conveniently, though many new bikes have shifters on the handlebars, even more conveniently. Avoid an unsuitable shifter position, such as at your handlebar-stem base; this position causes the rider to rise up for every shift. If your bike's shifters are at such a position, install new ones, say about a quarter way down the downtube.

Additional Component Concerns

On new bikes, watch for extras and ideal tire and saddle design and structure. The extras to watch for include attached accessories like racks, toe clips, bike computers, and water bottles and cages (all covered in the next section of this chapter). Obviously, the inclusion of any of these increases a bike's bargain-status. You'll want wider tires, say, 1¼"—Kevlar-belted tires last long and resist punctures. A hard-shell saddle is inappropriate for touring; get a slightly padded, anatomically shaped leather one. When purchasing your bike from a shop, request that they install the saddle of your choice.

Bikes Specifically for Women Cyclists

Standard bikes are not unisex in design. The old style "lady's bike" without a cross-tube has a weakened frame and does not address women cyclists' special needs. Generally, women have shorter arms and torsos, smaller hands and feet, and a different pelvic structure than men. Standard bikes built without regard for these physical differences can cause women cyclists undue discomfort. Bikes specifically designed for women feature shorter cross-tubes, smaller handlebars and brake levers and toe clips, and anatomically shaped saddles. Several manufacturers now offer such bikes. The innovator in the field, Terry Precision Bicycles (Appendix 2), manufactures a variety of gender-specific bikes and components and will mail you an informative catalog upon request.

Mountain and Cross Bikes

If you own a mountain bike or might get one for your tour—happy trails! With low gearing, wide tires, cantilever brakes, and a durable frame built for rough-road comfort, mountain bikes possess many touring bike qualities. One disadvantage is that the handlebars allow only one hand position, but you can buy handlebar extensions that partially remedy this. Also, the smaller wheel diameter means slower forward progress per pedal revolution, and replacement tires are hard to find in some areas. The main advantage is their any-road/off-road knobby tires. For tours with lots of side excursions down unpaved roads or global tours through less-developed lands (take a spare tire!), mountain bikes excel.

A decent compromise between mountain bikes and touring bikes are "cross" bikes. These too typically come with single-position handlebars. Their tires are fairly wide, though less so than mountain bikes', but are standard sized (27" or 700cm) in diameter. With suitably sturdy frames, low gearing, and an attractive price range, cross bikes are tour-worthy.

I have not discussed tandems or recumbents or unicycles or three-wheel bikes or. . . .You can tour on any bike that you want to; just remember the general principles discussed here, and apply them as you can.

Purchase Strategies

When shopping for a new bike, check first at local bike shops. That way, you can benefit from on-the-spot advice, free attachment of accessories, help with sizing and adjustments, the opportunity to negotiate price, and personal attention should anything go awry.

Other sources of new bikes are mail-order dealers and department stores. Major mail-order dealers (Appendix 2) will gladly sell you a quality bike at a decent price, but you then forfeit those significant benefits of dealing with a local shop. Although department-store bikes lure with

even lower prices, they prove a false value over the long road. First off, you lose most of the advantages of dealing with a bike shop. More importantly, most department-store bikes are inferior in design and construction and altogether inadequate for touring. The frames are generally heavy, and fragile at the cheaply welded joints. Mechanical breakdowns of every sort lurk all about these bikes. If you need to buy a bike on limited funds, better to hunt down a good used bike than to buy a new one at K-Mart or Wal-Mart or X-Y-Z Mart.

For used bikes, try bike shops, classified ads, bulletin boards, police auctions, swap meets, and garage sales. In buying a used bike from a bike shop, you gain many of the advantages of buying a new bike there, but will likely pay more than you would at one of the other sources. For police auctions (unclaimed "found" and stolen bikes), inquire at the station for time and place; you can likely examine the bikes beforehand.

Wherever you buy a used bike, examine it closely first. Look for the ideal touring-bike qualities discussed in this chapter: Does it have a stretched-out frame? low gearing? a good saddle? any attached accessories? Is it fairly light? How are the wheels' condition—do they spin true? How well do the brakes and the gear-shifting system work? Check for stress fractures on the frame, especially at the joints; chipped paint or a wrinkled appearance will clue you to a fracture; do not buy a bike with a fractured frame!

Remember that many bikes not specifically designed for touring possess touring-bike qualities. Look for them. If your new used bike is lacking in some way, improve it. Replace a ragged or hardshell saddle with a touring one, high gearing with low gearing, steel wheels with aluminum wheels, skinny tires with wider tires, badly placed shifters with strategically placed shifters. If you buy a used bike but lack mechanical know-how, have a mechanic thoroughly examine it prior to your tour.

Remember, *nearly any mechanically sound bike that fits you will suffice.* Did I mention the young woman I met on a Texas backroad who was cycling across that broad state—by unicycle?

For further information, consult a book specifically about bicycles. Three good ones: *Touring Bikes: A Practical Guide*, by Tony Oliver (Trafalgar), *The New Bike Book*, by Jim Langley (Bicycle Books), and *The Complete Mountain Biker*, by Dennis Coello (Lyons & Burford).

Attachments

The things that you might attach directly to your bike include water-bottle cages, racks, a lighting system, reflectors, a pump, a lock, toe clips, an odometer or bike computer, a tube-protection system, a "Flickstand," handlebar pads, mirrors, a horn or bell, fenders, a saddle pad, and a safety flag. Figure 2 shows the positioning of some of these. When you buy a bike from a bike shop and buy any attachments at the same time, ask the shop to attach them for you. It bears repeating that a number of these may come already attached to a new bike. Other low-cost sources include companies listed in Appendix 2 (order Performance's and Bike Nashbar's free catalogs) and, for some things (I'll identify these), department stores.

When attaching these yourself, follow the manufacturers' instructions and make sure that the connections are secure. To protect your bike's paint, insert a strip of rubber, such as a strip of inner tube or a tire patch, between the bike frame and any clamps or brackets.

Essential Attachments

You may ride tired awhile or hungry awhile, but do not ride thirsty! Well-equipped touring cyclists carry at least two **water bottles (with cages)**, three if touring through parched, sparsely populated regions. Quality water bottles and cages are inexpensive from bike shops and mail-order dealers. Avoid the slightly less costly department-store versions—the cages eventually fall apart and the bottles eventually spring leaks. Black water bottles absorb the sun's rays, warming your water, which will warm quickly enough without help! Finally, since a filled quart bottle weighs about two pounds, keep only one filled when in populated areas.

A quality **rear rack** will support much of your equipment weight, and should do so without swaying and without a breakage risk. Department-store models cost only about ten bucks, but these are heavy and unstable, and they pose a breakage risk; with a tiny bank account and

FIGURE 2

❶ rear rack
❷ water-bottle cages
❸ pump
❹ toe clips
❺ Flickstand
❻ handlebar pads
❼ front rack (low rider)

tinier tour-time load, you might chance one—but I wouldn't. It's best to get a quality one constructed of aircraft aluminum or a similarly strong, light material. They utilize either a three- or four-point attachment to your bike; all else being equal, a four-point attachment is more stable. Racks are sold by bike shops and mail-order dealers for about $30 or so. "Blackburn" dominates the field, not accidentally.

Whether or not you plan to pursue the pleasures of tranquil road night-riding, take a **lighting system**. After all, you might get "caught out" after dark at some point. Besides, when your road surface is smooth and traffic is nil, when fireflies flash and stars twinkle, you might find a night ride alluring.

Vistalite

For your **taillight**, you want an attention grabber. "Vistalite" tail lights reign superior in this category. Available from equipment dealers for $10 or so, the red or amber Vistalite's flashing action grabs drivers' attention from a distance, and the Vistalite gets up to 300 hours use from a pair of AA batteries. Other than Vistalites, any tail light that flashes or moves, such as a leg-band light, will do.

The best type of **headlamp** for touring is a detachable one that fits on a handlebar-mounted bracket. These serve double duty as a camp light. Bike shops and mail-order dealers stock a variety of models, starting at about $15. The ones with the super-bright Krypton or halogen lamps are more expensive, but worth it if you've the money and plan to night-ride often. A dirt-cheap double-duty option: devise a handlebar bracket for your camp flashlight with hose-clamps or velcro.

One other worthwhile lighting option is a **generator system** with a front and a rear light. As you travel down that road via your own power, you can also illuminate it via your own power. Generator systems eliminate the hassle, expense, and unpredictability of worn-down batteries (especially important when touring through parts of the world where replacement batteries are scarce). These environmentally sound lights start at about $10 (department stores), and go on up to brighter, more sophisticated, more expensive models at many bike shops. The biggest, but hardly insurmountable, objection to generator systems is that they add drag to your rear wheel; minimize this by installing yours so that friction is barely enough to spin the gyro.

Lights or no lights, you can't have too many **reflectors**. Most traffic laws require at least a rear one. Reflectors on your spinning spokes and pedals make swell attention grabbers. Go ahead—overdo it on these!

For about $15 or so you can purchase a reliable, lightweight **hand-pump** that attaches to your frame. Zefal is and has been the dominant brand, though other reputable companies (Blackburn, Performance) make quality pumps, too. Avoid the spare-change department-store versions constructed of cheap plastic and utilizing a detachable hose between the pump and your tire valve; that hose will spring a leak. Suitable pumps like Zefal's are constructed of alloy or high-impact plastic, hook-up directly to your tire valve, and prove reliable pump after pump.

Did I mention my bike was stolen in Las Vegas? Did you know that L.A. once had a law specifically prohibiting the gunning down of bike thieves? In short, perhaps your best "**lock**" is an avoidance of American cities! Besides that, take a simple lock (wrapped around your seat post while riding) to deter amateur thieves, and always keep your bike within sight. Park it in front of that homey cafe's window; wheel it into that grocery store or campground restroom; keep it near while you snooze, perhaps with bungee cords from it to a tent pole or your pillow. Shift it into high gear prior to parking it; few thieves could hop onto a loaded bike in high gear and pedal off without tottering to the sidewalk. Use bungee cords, cable ties, or electrical tape to secure detachable attachments. Then, relax: Most thieves are far lazier than you!

Optional Attachments

Toe clips are optional but strongly recommended. By keeping your feet on the pedals throughout the pedaling cycle, they increase your pedaling efficiency. Most new quality bikes come pre-equipped with toe clips; bike shops sell add-on toe clips for about $10. They're worth it. Not recommended: clip-less, cleated pedal systems requiring special shoes that are worthless off of the bike, meaning you'd have to carry an extra pair.

A very simple **odometer** costs a few bucks, some complex, multi-function **computers** over a hundred bucks, and you've numerous options between those extremes. My own touring tastes urge me to leave numbers and statistics at home, as much as possible anyhow, but perhaps yours differ? Your choice, completely optional.

Also optional, but recommended, is some type of **inner-tube protection system**. Your first line of defense against tube-molesting puncture-demons is a set of good puncture-resistant tires, such as those with a Kevlar belt. Your next line of defense is the use of either **tire liners**

("Mr. Tuffy" is standard) or **self-sealing tubes**. Tire liners—hardy, no-nonsense polyurethane strips that insert between your tube and tire and admit no puncture demons—await you at bike shops and department stores, less than ten bucks a pair. Self-sealing tubes—yes, just that—are sold by many bike shops and a few department stores; they cost nearly twice as much as tire liners and add about the same amount of justifiable weight to your rolling wheels. So called "puncture-resistant" tubes are less costly but make a poor compromise; they resist only the milder puncture-demons!

Flickstand

If "**Flickstand**" sounds suspiciously like "kick-stand," that is no mistake. They effectively replace kickstands on weighted touring bikes, which leave standard kickstands useless. You'll lean your bike a lot—against buildings, fences, lampposts, etc. The weight on your front wheel often causes it to kick out, though, sending your two-wheeled buddy to the cruel pavement. Installed beneath your downtube, a Flickstand flicks out and holds your parked front wheel straight and sincere. Nice? Ten bucks or less at bike shops.

A **front rack** is not essential but could prove useful. Although most touring cyclists use only rear saddlebags, many use front ones too, and this necessitates a front rack. (Saddlebags are discussed in the next section.) Front racks come in two styles: standard (like rear racks but smaller) and "low riders" (Figure 3). Some cyclists prefer standards, mainly because low riders do not provide you with a rack-top on which to place items; whether or not you take front saddlebags, you could carry a relatively bulky yet light item like your sleeping bag on a standard front rack. Low riders are used more often, though, because they keep the weight low and centered over the front axle.

For every hour that your feet spend on the pedals, your hands spend an hour on the handlebars, so consider taking some type of **handlebar pads**. The foam ones sold by bike shops and department stores for around five bucks will usually wear thin midway through a long tour. More durable and very comfortable, gel pads like those made by Spenco cost about ten bucks at bike shops. A low-cost, fairly comfortable, equally durable alternative: obtain refrigerator insulation tubing from an appliance store for free or for mere change, cut the length to fit, slit one side lengthwise, slide it onto your handlebars, and secure it with tape. It will pad your paddies for the length of your tour.

FIGURE 3

❶ rear saddlebags
❷ rucksack (containing tent, sleeping bag and sleeping pad)
❸ seat bag
❹ handlebar bag
❺ front saddlebags

Briefly, additional attachments, entirely optional, include **mirrors, a horn or bell, fenders, a seat pad,** and **a safety flag**. I don't use any of these, though a mirror is useful when in traffic, fenders when in rain, a seat pad when on bumpy roads, and the plastic whiplike flag pole when confronted by obnoxious dogs. If you take a horn, be aware that a New Mexico law did or does require that it produce a "harmonious sound" (perhaps get a French horn and take lessons before heading that way?). None of these items cost or weigh much, so I will not argue against taking any of them.

Bags

The main functions of the bags you'll take include distributing and transporting equipment, and protectioning it from the elements. Making you appear hip and stylish costs more and is not a main function, but is an option, an economy-boosting one at that. Figure 3 shows the standard placement of outer bags.

Essential Bags

Your **rear saddlebags** (often called panniers) hold much of your equipment, mile after mile, day after day, so choose carefully and emphasize durability. If you take along the optional front saddlebags, they will help carry the load; otherwise, your rear saddlebags are mobile-home to most equipment items. Decide how much capacity you'll need, and *then* shop for them. Their wide price range stretches from about $25 per small, basic pair to over $100 per large, luxurious pair. Major cost factors include size, number of compartments, and complexity of construction (not always a virtue). Compartments are not essential, but are convenient for organizing gear within the bags. The material of saddlebags is typically some variation of Cordura nylon; canvas is sometimes used, but it's heavier. With larger carrying capacity, multiple compartments, and a pleasing appearance, the expensive bags might justify their price to you. Still, I and others have toured cross-continent with relatively small (650 cubic inches per side), single-compartment saddlebags that cost only $25 or so.

Wherever they stand in the price spectrum, characteristics of *all* adequate saddlebags include water repellency, secure attachment to your rack, internal stiffeners to keep them out of your spokes, and rain flaps over the zippers. Only the larger bike shops will have as extensive a selection as the mail-order dealers, but bike shops more often offer the less expensive but still suitable ones.

Your **handlebar bag** will carry your while-riding snacks, various small odds and ends, need-em-quick items like your camera, and your in-use map—up top. Do avoid carrying too much weight in your handlebar bag, though, as it is at a high center of gravity. Quality ones range in price from around $15 to over $40, with size the main price factor. The qualities to look for: water repellency, internal stiffeners, outer mesh pockets, a transparent map-sleeve on top, an opening on the rider's side for easy access to the contents, stable and secure attachment to the bike, and a frame that allows finger space between the bag and the handlebars. Most bike shops and all mail-order dealers carry a selection of these. Department-store versions are usually too flimsy and nondurable, and utilize a poor attachment scheme. If you ride a smaller bike, try the bag on prior to purchase; on a small bike, a large handlebar bag might not fit within the handlebars and might drag on the front wheel (a front rack or fender solves that latter problem).

Later in this chapter we'll discuss your "Kits"— repair, bath, first aid, and chow. For each, you'll need an appropriately sized, securely closing **kit bag**. I use ziploc freezer bags for my chow and first-aid kits and a cloth drawstring bag for my repair kit. Since I sometimes carry my bath kit into cafes (more about that practice later), I stash it in a fairly attractive "shaving kit" type of bag.

Use **miscellaneous bags and baggies** for organizing your gear and keeping it dry. I like to use ziploc freezer bags for small items and thin trash bags for clothes. Take a spare trash bag for general use.

Optional Bags

Like a front rack, **front saddlebags** are optional. They do increase your carrying capacity and allow better front-to-rear weight distribution. Still, many bike tourists, including round-the-world ones, go without. You're trying to minimize weight and bulk anyhow, right? Because it's your *steering* wheel, you especially need to minimize weight and bulk on your front wheel, and loaded front saddlebags sabotage both aims. If you do use them, take small, single-compartment ones with the rear saddlebag qualities discussed above.

As in Figure 3, carry your tent, sleeping bag, and sleeping pad on top of your rear rack. A snugly fitting **stuff sack** will secure these items tightly together and protect them from the elements. They cost little at outdoor-gear retailers and department stores.

Completely optional are a **seat bag** and a **backpack**. I sometimes take a small seat bag for my tool kit, sometimes a small backpack for short end-of-day grocery hauling. Avoid carrying any substantial amount of weight on your back, though, as it would hinder your riding stability.

If during this babbling about bags, bags, and bags, you wondered, "Hey—what about sleeping bags?", that's coming up in the section on. . .

Camping Gear

For camping, equip yourself for comfort, but leave the ice chest and hatchet at home. Travel light! I know a weekend bike-camper who, on his first outing, packed a canvas tent with thick steel stakes. When his campside companion commented that these seemed a tad heavy for the occasion, he confidently replied, "No problem!", then pulled out a businesslike hammer—for pounding in the big stakes. Now experienced, he uses small, plastic tent stakes and his "hammer" is a rock found at the campsite. He now rides—not walks—his bike up hills.

Sleeping outdoors is a fine and fitting way to cap a day spent outdoors. Whether you'll camp every night or on occasional nights, at campgrounds or in the bush, put thought and care into your equipment selections. Choose small, light and functional. Especially if price is a factor, shop around. Among mail-order outfits, the ones in Appendix 2 generally have the best prices and cycling-relevant selections (request REI's and Campmor's catalogs). Outdoor-gear stores are another good source, department stores another, for certain simple, common knickknacks, anyhow. You'll find some useful things around the house—a length of cord, an old pocket knife, perhaps almost everything if you're a backpacker.

Essential Camping Gear

A Tent. You might not use your tent every night out, but when the sky rains or the night-breeze chills or the mosquitoes swarm, a good tent justifies its cost and weight. For $100-plus (sometimes plus plenty), you can purchase an exceptional one- or two-person tent that meets these standards: less than four pounds, compact when packed, durable double-stitched seams, leak-proof, condensation-resistant, stable in wind, reinforced floor, mosquito netting, and rain fly. Because of their durability, such tents are ideal for extremely long tours in which camping is a key element. A look through the REI and Campmor catalogs will familiarize you with the wide variety of high-quality tents, their features, and their price range.

If the price of such tents dismays you, find solace in the low price of common A-frame tents. Available from department stores for $30 or less, these perform well for most bike tours. Many seasoned bike tourists use them, and that includes me. Besides their attractive price, they too pack compactly, weigh only about four pounds, have mosquito netting and reinforced floors, and are fairly stable in wind when securely staked. Use the $70 or so that you save by buying an A-frame tent to buy some of the other equipment discussed in this chapter.

Some truly adventurous cyclists save even more money, weight, and bulk, by using a tube tent or a simple tarp. Not me: driving rain, insect swarms, chilling winds. . . .

If you do spend top dollar on any one piece of camping gear, make it your **sleeping bag**. Although you may not use your tent every night out, you will use your sleeping bag every night out. Choose your bag for low weight, packed compactness, and adequacy for anticipated night temperatures. The best touring bags have synthetic fill, weigh three pounds or less, and are tapered to fit your body's shape. The cycling and camping equipment dealers in Appendix 2 sell such bags for between $70 and $125. Unless you'll tour through high elevations, near one of the polar regions, or in the "fourth" season, a three-season bag with a comfort rating between 20 and 40 degrees will do. For my own tours, I bought a "Slumberjack Solite Quallofil tapered Hiker-Biker" from Campmor for about $70, a price that is holding steady. Only 2¼ pounds and comfortable down to 40 degrees, these are very popular among bike tourists. If you cannot afford such a bag and must take one from around the house, just make it the lightest one you can find, and keep it dry while touring.

Under your sleeping bag at night goes a **sleeping pad**, important for sound sleep. Air mattresses are relatively expensive and heavy and can spring a leak; they're then worthless until patched, but isn't the patching of punctured tubes enough? "Open cell" pads are bulky and absorb water like a sponge. I recommend a water-repellent, ½" thick, closed-cell pad. Visit an outdoor-gear store; have them cut you a pad that is ¾ the length of your body; give them a few bucks and walk out the door; whistle all the way home, then check "sleeping pad" on your equipment checklist.

Remember that a detachable bike headlamp serves double duty as your **camp flashlight**. Otherwise, get one, any one you can afford that is small and lightweight. One of those two-dollar plastic ones will suffice, but be aware that an external switch can switch on in your bags as you pedal along, singing to yourself and waving at strangers, unaware that your batteries are wasting away. With such a flashlight, remove your batteries during the day; better yet, get a flashlight with a less vulnerable or a more stubborn switch.

Self-explanatory essential camping items: a **camp knife, insect repellent,** and a section of **cord/rope.** Remember the double-duty concept when considering knives like the Swiss Army type, with can-opener, scissors, and and other little extras.

Optional Camping Gear

A backpacking type of **cookstove** is optional but highly recommended. The benefits of hot, economical meals in the evening and hot drinks in the morning are self-evident. Also, with a stove you can boil questionable water for safe drinking. Possible reasons not to pack a stove include cost, weight, and bulk.

If you do take a stove, choose a light, single-burner unit that uses a common fuel. Look in the backpackers' section of outdoor-gear stores or browse through the catalogs. For between $25 and $75 you can obtain a compact stove that weighs a pound or less, not including fuel (about another pound). If you tour with others, you can distribute the stove and fuel weight among riders. An extremely economical option is canned fuel—yes like Sterno, but without the steel fold-out stove; there are lighter, still inexpensive alternatives constructed of wire or thin aluminum.

A cookstove is closer to "Essential" for global touring. The water-boiling function might come in handy outside of Europe and North America. (We will discuss water purifiers in the next section under "Chow Kit.") Availability of fuel varies from land to land; MSR's "Whisperlite Internationale" rises to the occasion by using any of several common fuels.

With a stove, you'll need **biker's kitchen items: cookware** (aluminum, no more than needed), **foil, cooking oil, pot-scrubbers**, and a **collapsible water container** for carrying extra cooking and cleaning water at day's end, ideally for short distances. You can add the smaller items to your chow kit. Take a **lighter or waterproof matches**, too—you'll want them anyhow on those nights when you seek the incomparable pleasures of sitting around a campfire. Also useful: **chips off a fire-starter log**, and a wire **"Pocket saw."**

Other things that you could take if you care to carry them: **a candle-lantern or a small candle, a pillowcase** cut to half length, an **inflatable "camper's pillow"** (better yet, use your clothes bag), a plastic **groundcloth**, and a **tent-repair kit**.

We'll discuss Youth Hostels later. If you'll stay at any while touring, you'll need to make and take a **"Sheet Bag"**—a sheet cut and sewn to fit around you, required for sleeping on Youth Hostel beds.

An informative if overly technical book about combining camping with cycling is *The Bicycle Camping Book*, by Raymond Bridge (Stackpole Books). Two outstanding backpackers' books with heaps of expert advice about choosing and using ultralight camping gear are *Back-*

TOSRV photo by Greg Siple

packing Basics, by Thomas Winnett, and *Backpacking, One Step at a Time*, by Harvey Manning. The latter book, an outdoors classic, is not only informative but very entertaining. Look for these and other camping titles at a library or bookstore.

Kits

The Repair, First Aid, Bath, and Chow kits form, respectively, miniature, simplified versions of your workshop, medicine cabinet, bathroom, and kitchen drawers. As with all equipment, take only what you'll need, in the smallest quantities practical—several bandages instead of an entire box, trial-size toothpaste instead of family- size, etc. Since your own needs, tastes, and common sense can guide you here, I'll keep commentary brief.

You can buy such kits prepackaged; however, for economy of both cost and weight, assemble your own. Some items you'll find around your home, others in stores' "trial size" sections. You can easily replace items as you deplete them while touring. Your pre-tour research for global touring will show that certain items, like tampons and toilet paper, are not commonly available everywhere; plan accordingly.

Repair Kit, Essential

Take a **patch kit, tire levers, screwdrivers** (phillips and standard), **pliers** with a wire-cutting function, **allen wrenches**, a **multi-fit wrench**, **spare nuts and bolts**, a **spare brake cable**, a **spare derailleur cable**, several **spare spokes** and a **spoke tool**, several **cable ties**, a half-roll of **electrical tape, chain lubricant**, a light **rag** and tube of **handcleaner**, a **12" strip of old tire**, and **the know-how to use the tools you take** (practice at home).

Typically made of hard plastic and available for a few bucks at bike shops, the tire levers help in removing a tire from its rim. You could instead use your aluminum camp spoon, but tire levers are light and cheap, and work best. Do not use your screwdriver to remove your tire, as it would puncture your tube.

Take the lightest and smallest usable versions of screwdrivers, pliers, and wrench. A good small crescent wrench will do, but bike-specific wrenches do better. Take only the sizes of allen wrenches you'll need. For chain lubrication, WD-40 will do, but it's not ideal (too thin); bike shops sell better chain lubricants.

Remove the wire from the edges of that strip of tire. You'll use it if you experience a blowout: when that happens, insert it beneath the damaged part of your tire to protect the new or patched innertube, inflate the tube, and then high-tail it to a bike shop. For touring through extremely remote areas, a **spare tire** is recommended luggage, and likewise if your tire size is not widely available where you'll tour.

Repair Kit, Optional

Optional items include a **spare inner tube**, a **chain-riveter** and **chain-link master**, a **freewheel removal tool**, a **pedal wrench**, an **air-pressure gauge**, an **"extra hand" tool**, a **sprocket wrench, cone wrenches, bottom bracket tools, grease** and **spare ball bearings**, and a **booklet-sized repair manual.**

Except for the spare tube, I've carried and needed none of these in thousands of miles of touring. If I took just one, I'd take the freewheel removal tool; after flat tires, bike tourists' second most common "breakdowns" are broken rear-wheel spokes, and a freewheel removal tool is usually necessary to replace them. As to the other tools, they cost money, and they add weight and bulk. If you depart with a mechanically sound bike, you'll not likely need them. Besides, you'll seldom be far from civilization and civilization everywhere has bike shops and bike mechanics—or, at the least, mechanically adept locals.

I do pack a spare tube and urge you to do likewise. Rather than fix every #!X*% puncture on the roadside and possibly fail to do so, I replace the #!X*% punctured tube with my spare and then patch the #!X*% one at the next convenient stop. It then becomes my new spare. Try that.

Maintenance and repairs are given further attention in Chapter 3.

Bath Kit, Essential

Pack **shampoo, conditioner, deodorant, nail clippers, cotton swabs, toothpaste/powder** and a **toothbrush,** a light **washcloth,** a **pocket mirror,** a **comb or brush,** a small, flattened roll of **toilet paper,** and **liquid soap** (preferably biodegradable.)

Essential if you wear **contact lenses:** your **case, solutions,** and possibly a **spare pair.**

Essential if you're a pre-menopause woman: **feminine hygiene items.** You can of course get them as you go, but do note that these are not readily available in all world regions.

Bath Kit, Optional

You could also take **premoistened towelettes, skin cream, cosmetics, a shaver.**

I haven't yet but may eventually take a "**Sunshower.**" These are plastic water bags with a shower nozzle. You fill the bag, hang it overhead, play your harmonica or eat a snack while the sun generously warms the water, and then shower under it. You'll sometimes find it hard to obtain a needed shower while touring, so consider this option. Basic Designs makes one weighing 11 ounces that is good for up to 7 minutes of showering, and a 3.5-ounce one good for a minute or two. Campmor sells these for about $12 and about $7, respectively.

First-Aid Kit, Essential

Pack **bandages, pain relievers, medical tape, antiseptic cream, baby powder** or **cornstarch, sterile gauze pads,** and an **all-purpose antibiotic.**

Of course, any prescribed medicines would also be essential, along with your refill order. For foreign touring, have your doctor use the generic term on the refill order.

First-Aid Kit, Optional

Possible additional inclusions are a **dental emergency kit,** a **needle, tweezers,** a **snake-bite kit, medications for minor ailments** that might occur, like athlete's foot and bug bites, **medications for not-so-minor ailments** that could occur on international tours, like diarrhea and malaria. For those minor ailments, buy the medication if and when you need it. For those not-so-minor ailments, research ahead of time and go prepared.

You might also pack a brief, basic **first-aid manual.**

Chow Kit, Essential

Take an aluminum or "Lexan" **spoon and fork** (though plastic ones, replaceable at fast-food joints, might suit you), a personally blended all-purpose **spice mix,** some good **multi-vitamins,** and a small **can opener**—the "scout" type is the lightest and smallest.

You can find small packets of salt, pepper, catsup, mustard, hot sauce, etc., at fast-food joints and convenience stores—they blotch your scenery, you pocket their penny goods, fair enough? I once met an earnest train-riding hobo who claimed that mixing a few free catsup packets with hot water results in palatable, belly-warming tomato soup; in a pinch, try it!

Chow Kit, Optional

Some type of **water purification method** is optional but recommended. You could use iodine, but it leaves a medicinal taste. Better are the various brands of widely available water-purification tablets. If you're planning a global tour and have the funds ($60 to well over $100), consider taking along a backpacker-size water filter. Available from REI, Campmor, and outdoor-gear stores, some are pocket-size and weigh well under a pound.

Clothing

When selecting your touring attire, consider riding comfort, packed weight and bulk, expected weather conditions, and visibility to motorists. Take as little as is practical. I prefer cotton for its comfort and light-ness, though some synthetics, such as spandex, also prove comfortable and keep you warmer when wet—a drawback to cotton clothing is that it'll chill you when wet. Bright colors are cute and increase your visibil-ity in traffic, not a bad combination.

You will likely tour during warm-weather months. If not, add to the below listings **cool-weather additions** like **leg tights, arm warmers, thermal underwear, full finger gloves, a jacket** or **parka,** and, possi-bly, a **balaclava** (face mask). In cooler weather, your upper body, hands, and feet will demand extra attention. Give it to them.

Essential Clothing

I take two pairs of **shorts,** two **tee-shirts/tank tops,** a **long sleeved tee,** three pairs of **socks,** three pairs of **underwear** (unless—better yet—my shorts have built-in liners), a **sweat suit, sunglasses,** simple **raingear,** and a suitable pair of **shoes.** Some touring cyclists pack even less clothing.

My shorts are usually loose, lined, cotton-blend cycling shorts, ex-tremely comfortable. Available in both men's and women's designs, these cost around $25 from Performance and Bike Nashbar. Both of these mail-order cycling stores have a wide variety of cycling clothes. I have also toured in comfortable cotton shorts from "around the house," but you should first wear such shorts on a long pre-tour ride to find out if they remain comfortable during long hours on the saddle; specifically, the seams may become increasingly irritating, if not downright hostile. Spandex shorts are indeed comfortable, but the standard skin-hugging type is a tad conspicuous, especially off of the bike. Think twice about wearing these through conservative regions where you'd rather be a guest than an entertainer.

Shoes suitable for touring fit well, have stiff soles, and are also com-fortable when walking. Performance and Bike Nashbar both sell cycling shoes with these features and more for around $40 and, of course, up.

Lately, I take a simple rain poncho or hooded windbreaker, and plan to find shelter when rains come. Ponchos are not suitable on a bike for long. For about $40, you can buy a made-to-pedal rainsuit, but on a fairly warm day you'd sweat your way to wetness in these, so what's the point? For more money yet (up to $100-plus), you can get a stylishly designed rainsuit with "breathable" Gore-Tex fabric, which presumably lets out the water vapor you create, but you still might get wet from sweat, and riding in the rain is still messy and hazardous. Unless you'll tour through lands of endless rain—say, Oregon or Ireland—consider taking some-thing cheap, light, and simple, and aim for a cozy cafe or a spot beneath a bridge when the world takes a shower.

Optional Clothing

Many touring cyclists also pack a **bra** or two, a **helmet**, and **off-bike formal wear**. I always take **cycling gloves,** but am listing them as optional because they are.

Women cyclists tell me runners' bras are comfortable and decrease chafing and perspiration dampness. Ranging in price from $15 to $25, these are sold by most activewear dealers, including the equipment dealers in Appendix 2.

Helmets are optional but *strongly recommended.* Seriously consider wearing one, especially if your tour's route includes many busy roads and urban areas. A wide selection, most of them light, attractive, and meeting accepted standards, awaits your cash, check, or credit card. The mail-order dealers' helmets range in price from $30 to $100. Cost-comparison shop at a local bike shop.

You might take a semiformal outfit for attending church services and/or dining at restaurants. If so, choose the lightest possible outfit. Such an outfit becomes essential if your tour will include visits to European cathedrals or excursions into lands where extreme modesty in clothing is the norm.

Cycling gloves pad your overworked palms and prevent hand slippage. Mine evolve into a second skin; I often sleep in them! Strongly recommended. Priced from $10 to $25, they come in various styles, all of them fine. Try them on before buying.

What else you could take or could leave at home: **booties**, a **headband/ bandanna, safety goggles**, and a **money-belt**. The goggles will keep nighttime bugs out of your eyes, and the headband or bandanna, sweat out of your eyes.

Two small children enjoy TOSRV in the comfort of a long trailer

TOSRV photo by Greg Siple

Odds and Ends

This section gathers together miscellaneous items. Most of them are small, and will fit into your handlebar bag. Use your creativity regarding the little things. The lines between essential and optional are hazy here, but I've drawn them anyhow and added a third category—"Global Tourist's Miscellanea."

Essential Odds and Ends

Don't leave home and hearth without your **maps, journal** and **pen/pencil, personal identification, emergency info. card, sunscreen, sunglasses, lip balm/chapstick**, and **bungee cords/luggage straps.**

That emergency info. card should state your medical allergies, religious preferences if any, and whom to contact in an emergency. Obtain adequate bungee cords or luggage straps to secure all loose equipment, and then carry a spare.

Optional Odds and Ends

Possibilities: **camera** and **film**, a small **compass**, a **portable radio/tapeplayer, a portable alarm**, a slender **book, "Halt!" type spray protection, water-flavoring mix**, light **fishing gear, membership/access cards** (bank, credit, clubs, etc.), **field glasses, breath-freshener drops**, a baggy of **safety pins, rubber bands** and **twist ties**, a **plastic magnifying glass** (for map reading), a **standard-sized sink plug**, a **disposable pen-light** as back-up, a **harmonica**. . . .

If for no other reason, pack a camera for photographing people met while touring. If you'll use any air transport, be aware that X-ray machines can sabotage camera film; have security hand-check it.

Make your own odds-and-ends list. I might as well tell you now that some experienced bike tourists take along their dogs, others take movie equipment, yet others take mini ham radios. (They've even started a club, Bicycle Mobile Hams of America. For information, write them at P.O. Box 4009, Boulder, CO 80306.)

Global Tourist's Miscellanea

All of these I strongly recommend for touring away from your native land. As your pre-tour research (Chapters 2 and 4) will show, most are absolutely essential. Here they are: your **passport with required visa stamps**; a **back-up ID card** stashed away; **international bank, credit and membership cards** (if any); **vaccination certificates** as required; **bank certificate of financial capability** as required for entry into certain lands; **prescription information in generic terms**; **phrase booklets** (or lists in your journal); and your **transportation tickets.**

For now, though, you are at home, fully equipped, and we should look at. . .

Loading the Bike

The strategies for the proper loading of equipment on a touring bike are mercifully few and relatively simple. Once you've learned them, load your bike for trial rides and—ideally—a weekend tour or two. That way, you will familiarize yourself with riding a loaded bike (next section), do an "educated" rethinking of your equipment selections, and redistribute your luggage as seems best.

In loading your bike, keep the weight low, maintain an even side-to-side balance, and aim for a ⅓ to ⅔ front-to-rear weight distribution.

By placing heavier items lower in your saddlebags, you'll lower your center of gravity and achieve better riding stability. Side-to-side balance is reached by carefully placing your items and rechecking for balance every time you repack. Hold the loaded bike straight and upright by its handlebars, then let go; a balanced bike will not quickly fall toward either side.

Riding stability is further achieved by placing about ⅔ of your weight in the rear, about ⅓ in the front. Your front wheel is your easily distracted steering wheel, and with too much weight there, strong sidewinds or lumps in the road will cause you undue upper-body strain and could cause you to tumble. The reasons you put *any* weight there are for convenience (handlebar-bag items), and to eliminate the skittishness caused by having nearly all weight in the rear. Let's say you minimized equipment weight and kept yours at about 30 pounds. First, let me congratulate you. Next, let me advise you to put about 20 pounds in the rear, about 10 pounds in the front. With front saddlebags, you could possibly carry more weight up front, but you definitely don't want much more than 10 pounds there.

Place your tent, sleeping bag, and sleeping pad on top of your rear rack, preferably within a stuff sack. Strap them tight; you don't want them to bounce, let alone fall off.

Finally, thoughtfully organize equipment within your bags for ease of access. Keep small need-'em-quick items in your handlebar bag, larger need-'em-quick items on top in your saddlebags. If you carry liquid cookstove fuel, keep it sealed and separate from food. Some cyclists carry their fuel bottle in their third water-bottle cage, not a bad idea. Systematically arrange equipment within your bags—for example, clothes always in one saddlebag and kits always in the other.

Pack your bags and take a spin. Adjust. Repack. Take another spin. Arrive at your own packing scheme, and try to stick with it.

Riding the Loaded Bike

Let's first review several basic cycling techniques, then the handling peculiarities of a loaded bike. After that, we can pull out our maps and start making plans.

Basic Cycling Techniques

Any time you ride, use your low gears to advantage. Starting from a stopped position, use your lower ("easier") gears and shift up as you reach higher speeds. Your "cadence" (the rpm of your pedals) should remain fairly steady at between 70 and 90. As you encounter hills or wish to decrease or increase your speed, adjust not your cadence but your gears. Avoid "pushing" in a high gear—that is inefficient and will strain your knees and lower back.

With toe clips, you can attain a high-cadence spinning motion: rather than only pushing on your pedals, you push and pull; as you get familiar with the technique, you begin to spin your pedals in a fast, smooth motion.

Adapt to rolling roads by changing your gears, not your consistent high-cadence spinning. When beginning a climb, shift down early, one gear at a time, never pushing yourself until you've reached your lowest gear. When approaching a stop, shift down so that you need not strain when you take off again. On long descents, shift steadily upward, and then leave it in your highest gear while coasting for maximum control should you need to suddenly swerve.

Riding a Loaded Bike

A loaded bike rides somewhat differently from an unloaded one. Specifically, riding is slower and more strenuous, especially up hills. You'll surely curse your loaded bike early on, but may eventually learn to love it; after a long tour, I feel incomplete riding without my equipment weight!

When ascending a hill, remember to shift down early—before you're forced to. If at some straining point you need to stand and pedal, fine, but avoid swaying side-to-side too severely. If you must get off and walk, fine again, enjoy the scenery. Your payoff is the downslope.

When approaching a stop at a high rate of speed, start braking early with short quick taps on your brake levers. A loaded bike with forward momentum stops more slowly than an unloaded one. Use your front and rear brakes about equally and at the same time. Avoid sharp turns and fast turns, and do not lean into turns nearly as much as you would on an unloaded bike.

When you're riding a loaded bike, sidewinds and road-surface irregularities also merit extra attention. Because of your bags, your wind resistance increases, most noticeably to sidewinds; use caution when in a sidewind. Potholes, road debris, and road edges also pose threats that increase with your bike's increased weight. Your maneuverability is lessened, so avoid obstacles before you're on top of them. On unavoidable bumps and drops, raise yourself from your saddle to protect your wheels.

Again, take trial rides on your weighted bike to experience its quirks and moods, also to rethink your equipment choices.

For further, detailed reading on cycling technique, try *Bicycle Gearing: A Practical Guide*, by Dick Marr (The Mountaineers), *A Woman's Guide to Cycling*, by Susan Weaver (Ten Speed Press), or any other relevant titles you find at your library.

At last, you've equipped your bike and know how to ride it. Grab a beer or a milkshake, and order a pizza or pop some popcorn, because now it's time for— 🚲

TOSRV photo by Greg Siple

Chapter Two:
Armchair Travel

Those who go down to the sea tell part
Of its story,
And when we hear them we are
Thunderstruck.
——Sirach

Journey over all the unverse in a map,
without the expense and fatigure of traveling,
without suffering the inconveniences
of heat, cold, hunger, and thirst.
——Cervantes

Although it is important that you thoroughly equip yourself, it is less important that you thoroughly plan your route. Some bike tourists do minimal pre-tour planning and mapping, and discover their roads and destinations en route. Others seek to know beforehand each road they'll ride down, each town they'll pass through, each campground or hotel or hostel they'll stay at. Most of us fall somewhere between those two extremes.

This chapter guides you into daydream-sparking Armchair Travel activities. The subchapters cover organizational help, mapping sources and strategies, research, and reading. Use the recommendations to get a little information or a load of information, whatever amount you're comfortable with, whatever amount you desire.

And, somewhere in there, you might round a corner and enter Armchair Travel Mode—you'll no longer be in the armchair but on a distant mountain road, at a hidden campground with a fire crackling, or in a tiny town's sole cafe where the daily specials are hospitality and charm.

This anticipatory pleasure will never be as vivid as when anticipating your first long tour, so enjoy it.

Organizational Help

When planning your trip, you can tap into the resources of dozens of helpful organizations, including cycling clubs, traveler's organizations, bike-tour operators, and American Youth Hostels-Hostelling International. Although planning and executing a long bike tour is primarily an individualistic affair, you can use these organizations' great wealth of resources to great benefit.

Chapter 4 discusses cycling and travel clubs in various world regions. Most of them sell cycling-specific and cycling-suitable maps and guidebooks at a discount to members, but also to nonmembers. Some will also give expert answers to specific questions about cycling in their region. For the U.S., try the Adventure Cycling Association (formerly Bikecentennial); for Canada, try the Canadian Cycling Association; for Latin America, try the South American Explorers Club; for Europe and beyond, try the Cyclists' Touring Club. You'll find these and others discussed in their respective sections of Chapter 4. They are your best sources of information about cycling in unfamiliar lands. Most of them are also nonprofit organizations, so enclose return postage when writing them for information.

On the other hand, commercial group-tour operators do it for the profit. They map your route (actually *their* route), arrange for your nighttime accommodations, blend you in with other cyclists, provide you with a tour leader, sometimes prepare your meals, and often carry your gear.

They also charge two to ten times what you'd spend on a do-it-yourself tour. In taking care of nearly everything, they take away much of the challenge, spontaneity, and sense of adventure so important in a do-it-yourself tour. Furthermore, by touring in a sizable group, you insulate yourself from the locals whose neighborhoods you ride through.

I'd recommend such tours only if you want guidance and companionship your first time out to gain experience and confidence for future do-it-yourself tours, or for touring through foreign lands that you're simply not willing to tour through on your own. Most national bike clubs provide members with directories of commercial tour operators. The back pages of cycling magazines teem with advertisements for pay-to-pedal tours heading nearly everywhere.

Of group tours, the most natural and least costly (funny how often that fortunate combination pops up) are those conducted by cycling clubs and Hostelling International chapters. If you're going to try touring with an organized group, try it with one of these.

One membership organization worth joining, especially if you'll tour in Europe, is American Youth Hostels-Hostelling International (AYH-HI). By joining your national chapter, you automatically join HI. AYH has about 220 hostels and a quarter-million members. Most North American hostels are concentrated near the coasts and in the spectacular mountain regions. Internationally, youth hostels are highly concentrated in Europe (where they originated), but they also span the globe—all continents, 70 countries.

Hostels offer low-cost dormitory-style accommodations typically set in major gateway cities, historic sites, and generally magnificent settings—in other words, areas you might cycle through. Besides beds, the typical hostel has showers, kitchen facilities, separate sleeping quarters for men and women, discount coupons for local restaurants and entertainments, and various other goodies. They exist to accommodate adventurous travelers like you.

The hostels themselves can delight. As an HI member, you might pedal up and settle down into a converted Victorian mansion, a century-old log cabin, a renovated lighthouse, an old Nantucket lifesaving station, a medieval castle on the Rhine River, a former royal residence in London, or an old cutter ship in Stockholm. Best of all, inside the hostels you'll find adventurers from widely scattered lands with travel tales to spike your juices, perhaps with tips about roads and regions yet ahead of you.

For members of *all ages*, overnight fees range from about 50 cents (India) to about $7 (most North American ones) and about $20 (New York City and Tokyo, so still a bargain.) As I write, the annual individual AYH membership fee is $25. Members receive a membership card accepted at hostels around the world and a comprehensive, illustrated guidebook to North American hostels (guidebooks to hostels worldwide cost a small sum). As long as you're lounging in your armchair contemplating possibilities, grab some stationery and write AYH for full details (American Youth Hostels, 733 15th St. NW, Suite 840, Washington, D.C. 20005). If you and your armchair are in Canada, write Hostelling International Canada (1600 James Naismith Dr., Suite 608, Gloucester, Ontario KIB 5N4, Canada).

Map Sources and Mapping Strategies

Plot a general course before you go. The bike tourist's ideal pre-tour mapping strategy involves charting a tentative main route and possible side routes, and knowing that mysterious roads lurk all around, waiting to lure unwary cyclists from their planned itineraries.

Cycling-Specific Maps

Although standard road maps are often sufficient, maps designed specifically for bicyclists are superior. The three main sources of cycling-specific maps are: 1) pedal-tested route maps from bike clubs like the Adventure Cycling Association; 2) books with maps and route descriptions, available from their publishers, bike clubs, and libraries; 3) free tourist-bureau cycling maps, sometimes with specific routes, other times with color-coded "Bicycle suitability" ratings of roads throughout their entire region. Quality cycling maps specify roads with both low traffic and high scenery. The low-traffic factor is significant.

There are hundreds of books that combine bike-route maps with route descriptions. They cover all areas of the U.S and Canada, much of Europe, and various countries throughout the world. Many are too bulky for a trimmed-down touring load, so borrow them from a library and transfer the useful information into your journal or onto your road maps. The best nonlibrary sources of such books are the bike clubs discussed in Chapter 4 and listed in Appendix 3 (Selected Book Sources) and Backcountry Bookstore, also listed in Appendix 3. Chapter 4 has reviews of books that cover regions for which good cycling information is otherwise scarce.

Tourist-bureau bike maps, variable in quality and usefulness but sometimes high in both, are free from a growing number of enlightened tourist bureaus, identified as such in Appendices 5, 6, and 7. When writing or calling a tourist bureau, communicate your cycling intent, and request cycling-specific information. Any tourist bureau with a North American office will send you English-language travel literature.

Some U.S. states have cycling maps available through their highway or traffic department or a "Bicycle Coordinator," but not from their tourist bureau. Not all of these maps are free. If you care to run them down, a good starting point is the Adventure Cycling Association's superlative membership publication, *The Cyclists' Yellow Pages*. However, before spending time and postage expense on this pursuit, take a walk while considering whether it's worth it. For a few states, perhaps yes, but for a multi-state tour, you might either see if an Adventure Cycling Association map or bike-route book shows your route, or else make do with what you do get from tourist bureaus.

Sources of Standard Road Maps

Speaking of tourist bureaus, they are your best source of free standard road maps. Tourist bureaus of all U.S. states and Canadian provinces, most European countries, and many countries worldwide, will send you a free road map of their region. Most North American tourist bureaus have toll-free numbers, meaning you need not even invest the time and cost of writing and mailing a letter. Other sources of road maps include libraries, bookstores, and travel stores such as those in Appendix 4. If a good atlas is beneath your armchair, you might start with it.

Regarding standard road maps for bike-touring purposes, the smaller the scale, the better. Small-scale maps show the backroads, and backroads you want. For small U.S states, very small countries, and areas where paved roads are few, standard road maps will do. Otherwise, seek out small-scale maps. A scale of 1:250,000 (1" equals 4 miles) is ideal. Outfits specializing in such maps for specific world regions get identified in Chapter 4. Try the mail-order travel stores in Appendix 4, too; some of them will hunt down requested maps they do not normally stock.

You could visit libraries along your route and photocopy their small-scale local maps (county road maps, for example). Other small-scale-maps-as-you-go sources include local tourist bureaus and branches of national automobile clubs. For global touring, note that AAA members have access to membership benefits of national auto clubs in other countries.

Routing off of a Standard Road Map

Cycling-specific maps, small-scale maps, and maps of areas where few roads are paved all present you with obvious routing options. When routing from a road map that is none of these, use the legend/key. Choose the roads identified as "secondary." All else being equal, roads that traverse relatively smaller towns will have relatively lighter traffic. Avoid main roads into large towns and cities. (For that matter, avoid unfamiliar cities when traveling on a bike.) A legend/key usually identifies camp-

AYH hostels are a great place to meet other travelers

AYH photo

grounds, historic sites, and public parks and forests. Unless they're so well known that they attract hordes of traffic, these merit your routing interest. Do not route your trip through U.S. national forests expecting a tranquil communion with nature's greenery, though, because logging trucks might blow you off the roads there.

If a road appears to wind and twist, look closer; it likely travels either beside a river or through rolling country. Both are superlative cycling settings.

When looking at a sparsely populated region like the U.S. southwestern desert, if it seems to have only interstate highways headed your way, don't despair. Federal U.S. law permits you to cycle an interstate when it is the only road going your way. Actually, with wide, paved shoulders and one-way traffic, rural interstates can prove safer and easier on your nerves than two-lane roads with two-way traffic and narrow shoulders.

In other words, a trafficked road with a wide, paved shoulder is far more suitable than a trafficked one without. Still, standard road maps do not indicate shoulders, much less shoulder width or condition. If a cycling-specific map or book shows where you want to go and you can afford it, consider getting it.

Research: Looking It Up

While in mapping you identify the route of your forthcoming journey, in researching you identify and learn about the people, cultures, facilities, and natural features along the route. Guidebooks, encyclopedias, and government sources provide basic information. Your nearest library is an ideal resource, especially if you're guarding your dimes and nickels.

Sleeping-Space Research

Because of your beautifully unpredictable day-to-day mileage, planning ahead for specific sleeping accommodations on specific nights is probably a waste of time. Still, through sleeping-space research you can identify suitable campgrounds and low-cost accommodations near your route to notate as "possible stay-overs."

If you're using cycling-specific maps or books, such information is likely included; otherwise, list "possible stay-overs" on your maps or in your journal. Bookstores, libraries, and travel stores stock a variety of campground guidebooks, but the best one for North America is the widely available Woodall's *Plan-It—Pack-It—Go*. It lists hundreds of campgrounds, state-by-state and province-by-province, with concise descriptions of physical setting, seasons open, number of sites, rates, facilities, and road directions to them. Recent editions give cycling information, including a good state-by-state bike-trail directory.

Through a Woodall's guide, I first learned of gotta-stop-there camp-grounds like City of Rocks, Sleepy Grass, Dipping Vat, and Bottomless Lake (New Mexico), Coyote Howls, Tortilla Flat, and Pioneer Pass (Arizona), Dripping Springs and Pogie Point (California), Lost Burro and Tall Texan (Colorado), Goose Point and Peaks of Otter (Virginia), Peepfrog, Beaver Meadows, and Moon Meadows (Pennsylvania). Sit down with your maps or journal and a comprehensive campground guidebook. Notate every campsite on or near your route, every campsite with an alluring name like, say, Lake Joy (Wisconsin). You can likely find Woodall's guides at a local library or bookstore, but if you can't, or if you have any questions, write to Woodall Publishing Co. (28167 N. Keith Dr., Lake Forest, IL 60045).

Other sources of sleeping-space information include tourist bureaus, bed-and-breakfast guidebooks, general travel guidebooks, and the youth-hostel directories. Most tourist bureaus will send you free, detailed guides to campgrounds and other accommodations in their state/province/region. The bed-and-breakfast guidebooks swarm at every library, bookstore, and travel store. The general travel guidebooks' accommodations listings are thorough, but they primarily cover congested areas; of the widely available guidebooks, the *Let's Go* and *Lonely Planet* guides best accommodate budget-minded and adventure-seeking travelers. If you plan to hostel during your tour, join AYH-HI, request their directories, and merge relevant listings with your routing information.

Once you start searching, you'll find more accommodations information than you can possibly use, and far more than you'll likely want. Zero in on the information you can use.

Additional sleeping-space possibilities, many of them refreshingly free and all of them spontaneously arrived at, are discussed in Chapter 3. Armed with the tips there and the guidebooks discussed here, you can sleep as soundly tonight as you will while touring—at, say, somewhere like Loafer Creek (California).

Cultural-Geographical-Weather Research

This kind of research looms largest on your priority list when planning a tour through unfamiliar foreign lands. Is the culture sexist? extremely conservative regarding modesty in clothing? What is the good local grub and where might you find it? Might you learn some common phrases in their language? Where are the mountains? When is the rainy season, the hot season, the cold season? Which way does the wind blow?

Good recent atlases and encyclopedias render general pictures. Tourist bureaus' facts will be accurate, but they'll only send you information aimed at attracting you their way. For deeper looks into cultures' hearts and souls, hunt down books about, and literature from, the cultures you'll visit. General travel guidebooks describe regions' basic cultural traits, natural features, and attractions both natural and not—for these and a variety of titles relevant to travelers, write the mail-order travel stores in Appendix 4.

But if you fear forming "preconceived misconceptions" about your destinations, if you prefer finding out the facts as you go, if all you care to know beforehand is the direction to there—well then, hop on your bike and ride!

Reading: Soaking It In

As long as you're solidly in your armchair with your tour solidly weeks or months away, as long as you're straining not your legs but your eyes, feed your anticipation by delving into cycling and outdoor skills literature generally, and personal bike-tour narratives specifically. First, we'll scan some reading possibilities primarily factual. After that, we'll examine some reading possibilities primarily wonderful.

Among magazines, the most relevant ones regarding bike touring are the member magazines published by the bike clubs discussed in Chapter 4. Among mass-market magazines, try the widely distributed *Bicycling* magazine. Issues frequently include a touring article or story. As bicycle touring gains mainstream interest, articles spring from all kinds of magazines. If interested in hunting them down, look in your library's *Readers Guide to Periodical Literature.*

For factual, practical reading matter, seek out books on bicycling basics, bicycle repair, camping techniques, campfire cookery, first-aid skills, stretching and self-massage methods, even "wilderness survival." (Stop, as I did, when you reach a tract about the emergency removal of one's own appendix. You'll never be *that* far from a town and physician! Besides, in case you've an urge to remove an appendix, Appendix 8 is a "tear & take" one just for you.)

Bike Tour Narratives

Secure and comfortable in your armchair, knowledgeable about bikes and bicycling and your touring destinations, you can enjoy some entertaining and enlightening book-length bike-tour narratives. I will here review those that I have read, enjoyed, and learned from. You could find others on library shelves and in bike-club catalogs. These books, especially the first four, make extremely rewarding reading. All of them will stimulate your visions of your own forthcoming tour and verbally illustrate the experiences open to those who visit the world via their own power.

This is *not* an overstatement: one of the finest books I've ever read is Barbara Savage's *Miles From Nowhere* (The Mountaineers). In vivid and delightful terms, Ms. Savage details—and at times joyfully exaggerates—

the trials and triumphs that she and her husband Larry experienced during a fantastic two-year, 23,000-mile tour through 25 countries. Colorful creatures and characters leap out of these pages and force you to smile. Written with both wit and wisdom, this book is a "must read" for bike tourists in waiting. If you've doubts about actually doing it, this book will dissolve them. Available from its publishers, the Adventure Cycling Association, Backcountry Bookstore, and well-stocked libraries.

The Long Ride (Stackpole) is Lloyd Sumner's book about his four-year, 28,000-mile bike trip all over the planet. Sumner left home on an old bike, without training, without preparing, with only $200 in his pocket. When no road went where he wanted to go, he left the road. Side excursions included canoeing, yachting, scuba diving, mountain climbing, ostrich riding, elephant riding. He was stalked by a leopard, charged by an elephant, chased by a rhino, marooned on an island. In the end, he states, "I have been stretched, in other words, stretched beyond any singing of it." Yet sing he does in this splendid book. Look for it at a library.

Another fascinating book, this one about a 40,000-mile tour spanning five continents, is *The World Up Close*, by Kameel B. Nasr (Mills and Sanderson). In a Himalayan village near the end of his odyssey, Nasr comments, "I came to be impressed by mountains, and mountains I saw, but it was human beings that penetrated my emotions." This insightful narrative is indeed very much about people met, in obscure settings throughout the world. It is also about the inner discovery and self-fulfillment that accompany any long bike tour. Like all touring narratives, it is also about occasional trials and troubles, and the overcoming of same. Swell reading, especially—but hardly only—recommended if you'll tour through Latin America, Africa, Asia, or the Mideast. Backcountry Bookstore carries it, or you can solicit your librarian's help.

If Walt Whitman were alive and cycling, he might write something like Mark Jenkins does in *Off the Map: Bicycling Across Siberia* (Wm.

TOSRV photo by Greg Siple

Morrow; paperback reprint, HarperCollins). Poetic Jenkins cycled the length of Russia with a group composed of fairly equal parts men and women, Soviets and Americans. That journey, incredible enough to begin with, included 800 miles through a roadless—yes, roadless—Siberian swamp. Splendid portraits of everyday Russians in isolated settings. As with all these narratives, and as you'll experience on your own tour, time off the bike produces memorable moments, too. Recommended, doubly so if your reading tastes tend toward the literary side. The Adventure Cycling Association and the Backcountry Bookstore sell it, and naturally you can try the library.

For a spirited tale of a transcontinental tour taken when both lifestyles and bike equipment were simpler, try *The Wonderful Ride* by George T. Loher (Harper & Row). This book springs from the journals of Loher, who, in 1895, meandered across the U.S. on a brakeless, single speed "Yellow Fellow." Traveling without maps, his "roads" included footpaths, wagon-train trails, and railroad tracks—between the rails, over the ties (Ouch!). The book bulges with anecdotes, observations, photographs, peculiar opinions, and background commentary from Loher's granddaughter. This book is easy to recommend, but hard to find—I found it at a library but have not seen it elsewhere.

Also worthwhile reading is *Changing Gears*, by Jane Schnell (Milner Press). At age 55, recently retired Schnell set off on a 12,000-mile tour around the perimeter of the U.S. Consisting of richly detailed daily journal entries, this book thoroughly describes the mile-to-mile, town-to-town, day-to-day bike-touring rhythms and realities. There's much description of small-town America. Especially recommended if you too will tour the U.S. perimeter or part of it.

Crackers and Peaches, same author and publisher, is again a daily journal describing a perimeter tour, this one around Georgia. Less ground covered, but for pure reading pleasure, it's perhaps the better of the two. For further information on either or both, send a request and S.A.S.E. to Milner Press (3842 Windom Place, N.W., Washington D.C. 20016).

Briefly, some others: *Two Wheels and a Taxi* (The Mountaineers) is a charming, zany tale by 70-year-old Virginia Urrutia, about her bike trip in Ecuador on a one-speed. *The Great Bicycle Caper* (Ageless Adventures, 8400 Menaul N.E., Suite A, Albuquerque, NM 87112), is Ed Wright's breezy, good-natured account of his ride across the southern U.S. at age 62. *Discovering America* (Lone Rider Productions, P.O. Box 43161, Tucson, AZ 85733) is Martha Retallick's spirited tale of her cycling adventures in all 50 states, with thoughtful tips for those planning a first-time bike tour. *One Time Around* (APT Publishing, 6103 Reo St., Toledo, OH 43615) is Alan Thompson's recounting of his year off from teaching high-school history spent (naturally!) riding around the world. For information about these four books, write the publishers. *Two Wheels*

...and here are some who toured.

Mark Connelly was a member of an Adventure Cycling Association TransAmerica tour. His group made a 90-day, 4,250-mile crossing of the United States from Yorktown, Virginia, to Astoria, Oregon.

Greg Siple, Adventure Cycling Association art director, pulled his 14-month-old son in a trailer from Missoula to Helena, Montana, accompanied by wife and mother, June Siple. "Our trip was only five days and 200 miles but it was plenty for Zane's first time on tour. He slept most of the time in the trailer and we made frequent stops for feeding and diaper changing. He was just learning to walk and enjoyed exploring every time we stopped. We stayed in motels two nights and camped the other two. Zane is six years old now and quite used to getting about in the trailer because we haven't owned a car since he was born."

Kate Brill and Charley Stevenson teamed up on their unique Counterpoint tandem to ride from Portland, Maine, to Seattle, Washington. As a change of pace, they boarded the 600-foot grain freighter Kinsman Independent in Buffalo, New York for an 80-hour passage to Superior, Wisconsin where they resumed bicycling. "Kate and I are both 21 years old and recent graduates of Williams College. Our parents were very apprehensive about this trip. They feared not because of our judgement, but rather because of random acts of violence which occur every day. They feared that we might fall prey to unkind and unthinking people. However, the vast majority of our encounters with people were extremely positive."

Italian cyclist Franco Nicotera successfully completed a 59-country round-the-world tour. At the time of this photo he had ridden 46,000 kilometers, had 185 flats, worn out 25 tires, taken 83 spills, had four accidents with cars, and in Thailand had been shot. After taking the bullet in the back he ran his assailant off with his pump. The umbrella was a modification for traveling in the hot parts of South Asia.

After a year and a half of planning, Dan and Amy Karns of Cleveland, Ohio, vacationed out west on their Franklin Tandem with a tour from Vancouver, Canada, to Jackson, Wyoming. Dan is a physician and Amy is an occupational therapist.

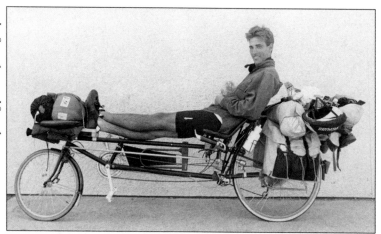

Joachim Pohl, 21, of Germany rode a Radius Recumbent on his rambling tour of the west, which began in Salt Lake City and took him to Los Angeles. The trip was a celebration of his completion of service in the army. "It was a wonderful vacation, but it is going to be the last of that sort of thing for a while. I am now studying law at the Eberhardt's Karls University. Money as well as time is lacking and a return to the wilderness of the American West must stay a dream."

Sixty-eight-year-old John W. Hathaway from Vancouver, Canada, began his serious cycling in 1953 with a 4771-mile Toronto to Vancouver tour. Since then he has made a series of notable treks including a 25-day crossing of Canada in 1957, and a 100-week, 50,000-mile, 52-country world tour in the early 1970s. When this picture was taken in the summer of 1993 he was in the middle of a 28,000-mile tour of the United States.

Adventure Cycling photo by Greg Siple

Ernest "Dwain" Williams had been on the road for a full year when this picture was taken and had no idea when his tour would end. As he wanders, he supports himself with the sale of balloon sculptures that he makes. He carries a supply of to three thousand balloons and can conjure up a couple hundred animals, creatures and characters. He is especially proud of his ballerina that brought him first prize at the Virginia State Clown Convention.

and a Taxi is also sold by The South American Explorers Club, discussed in Chapter 4.

If with weary eyes you set the books down and switch the stereo on for some on-the-road-again kind of music, that too constitutes Armchair Travel. So do late-night nature-channel specials about far-flung lands and cultures. So do deep, sweet dreams of smooth, tranquil roads rolling through forested countryside, wind calm, air temperature just right, you no longer page-flipping, but pedal-spinning. . . . 🚲

Chapter Three:
The Road Ahead

Henceforth I ask not good fortune, I myself am good fortune,
Henceforth I whimper no more, postpone no more, need nothing:
Done with indoor complaints, libraries, querulous criticisms,
Strong and content I travel the open road.
——Walt Whitman

I didn't have the time nor desire for a lengthy and rigorous
training schedule. Instead I adopted the rather questionable rationale
of saving my strength for the trip.
——Ed Wright, in *The Great Bicycle Caper*

This chapter answers questions that might otherwise distract you as you anticipate your upcoming journey. You'll likely wonder about physical conditioning, potential hazards, treatment by strangers, daily costs, places to sleep, what to eat, mechanical trouble, keeping yourself clean, climate and terrain extremes, dogs and other creatures, aches and pains and itches, keeping in touch with those at home, and coping with unpredictable on-the-road blues.

Answers are forthcoming, but first remember that the most important equipment is within yourself: your big heart, your open mind, your persistence, your adaptability, and, especially, your sense of humor. Life on a bike in unfamiliar territory will test you and sometimes irritate you, but it will also coax out inner qualities that, once activated, will endure to enrich your life and your outlook.

What kind of shape should I be in?

Good enough shape to attain great shape. The rigors of all-day everyday riding on a weighted bike will transform your body into an athletic marvel. Your pre-tour aim is to prepare yourself for those rigors. By doing so, you'll minimize physical discomfort—and the urge to "quit this silly endeavor"—on your initial days out.

Riding your bike is the best training activity, better yet when you ride it weighted. On-bike training is an enjoyable way to condition your cycling muscles and your food-to-energy system; it is also the *only* way to accustom your back, hands, and rear-end to all-day riding. If you're not now a cyclist, start with 20–25-mile days several days a week, and increase that distance by 10–15 miles each week until you can comfortably ride over 60 miles in a day. Your riding speed is unimportant during these rides. When you can comfortably handle 40–50-mile days, start adding increasing amounts of weight to your saddlebags (I use encyclopedias or equipment). This will further strengthen your cycling muscles and familiarize you with the effects of equipment weight.

Other than cycling, any aerobic activity is beneficial. If you've any doubts regarding your overall health, especially your cardiovascular health, visit a physician first. Finally, know that many long-distance bike tourists began their first tours as recovering couch potatoes but ended them as world beaters.

What about the use of planes or trains or buses?

If you begin or end your tour far from home, you'll use one of these to transport yourself and your equipment to/from your starting/ending place. Use your own preferences and budget in choosing one. Inquire beforehand about their bike-carrying policies. Most buses and trains accept boxed bikes as luggage, either for a small (say, $10) fee, or for free. Most airlines will carry your boxed bike as luggage on international flights at no charge, but often charge a relatively large fee on domestic flights.

Use a bike box to transport your bike. You can sometimes purchase a box from the air or train line, but your cheapest—often free—source is a bike shop: call and ask!

Preparing your bike for boxing involves some simple disassembly. Remove the wheels, seat, and seat post. Remembering that the left pedal has a left-hand thread, remove the pedals, too; should you need a pedal wrench, they cost little at bike shops. Loosen your handlebars, point the curve downward, and turn them sideways. This disassembly should allow you to fit your bike into the box. To protect vulnerable components like spokes and derailleurs, place padding (newspaper, cardboard, whatever) or other, less destructible equipment around them. Reinforce the box with cut-to-size wood blocks, and place one between the front fork dropouts to prevent bending. With some additional effort, you could fit much of your equipment in the box; you could then carry on small valuables and items needed en route in your saddlebags.

Do make certain the box is securely taped and clearly identified as yours.

For global touring, motorized transport obviously plays a larger role. Seek out the best trans-ocean travel bargains. Many countries have more extensive rural public-transport systems than does the U.S. Like the cyclist-accommodating Eurail system (See Chapter 4), foreign train and bus systems often carry unboxed bikes for little or no extra charge. Detailed information about a country's transport system is included in any good travel guidebook for that country.

If you've a lengthy ride or flight to your tour's starting point, consider reserving a hostel space or motel room for when you arrive; that way, you'll begin your tour sufficiently rested.

Is it safe and enjoyable to tour alone?

Yes to both of these. Many long-distance bike tourists go solo. By going it alone, you get to pedal at your own pace, you have the freedom to choose stop-overs and side-tracks without dissension, and you stand a far better chance of meeting locals. Indeed, when you wheel your loaded bike into a backwater hamlet, you'll find yourself not alone but the center of attention!

Touring with a partner or two has several benefits, though. Mutual support is one, "safety in numbers" another, the sharing of the weight-load and campground/motel fees yet another. Also, the sharing of spectacular experiences with loved ones can heighten your appreciation of both the experiences and the loved ones.

On a long tour, unfortunately, loved ones can quickly become loathed/despised/hated ones—a definite disadvantage! Compatibility is perhaps as essential on a bike tour as in a marriage. You need to match in personality, budget, tastes, physical condition, preferred riding speed, and riding aims and goals. If you tour with another or others, agree beforehand about speed, daily mileage, destinations, etc. Plan on occasional compromises and occasional nerve flares.

If, like Thoreau, you've "Never found the companion that was so companionable as solitude," a solo tour will suit you well. For safety's sake, steer clear of confrontations (for example, don't shout curses at rude drivers), and avoid weekend-night country roads, which can have party animals in big metal machines. Global tourists need to research potential trouble spots. Although I've heard of women safely touring alone nearly everywhere, for touring through a sexist culture a partner would make for more tranquility. *Any* solo tourists with persistent fears of night creatures should sleep at organized campgrounds or indoors.

Whether you tour alone or with a riotous mob, when you awake safe and sound and eager to ride off, your concerns will include. . .

What about dangerous road conditions?

To minimize dangers, know your basic rights, increase your visibility, and carefully choose your roads. In North America and most of the world, you theoretically have the same road rights and responsibilities as motorists. Exceptions: you are expected to ride near the road edge when in traffic, and you are denied access to most interstate-type highways. You are *not* a second-class citizen on public roads, so do not ride timidly. Make yourself highly visible with brightly colored clothing and equipment and strategically placed lights and reflectors. Most importantly, choose roads with the least traffic or, failing that, roads with the widest shoulders. When in doubt, ask local residents—bike-shop personnel naturally impart the best advice.

When caught on a busy road, ride cautiously but not timidly. Ride in the same direction as traffic, near—not on—the road-edge. Watch ahead for debris, potholes, glass shards. If your bike has knobby tires, you might try riding the soft shoulder of a busy road, but otherwise avoid the road-edge dropoff. When in heavy two-way traffic on a narrow two-lane road, follow the white edge-line only when that allows plenty of space for passing automobiles; otherwise, take the whole lane. Claim the whole lane on fast descents, too.

Busy roads are not only dangerous but mood-destroying. Keep your cool intact and resist flipping "the bird" at rude drivers. Pull over for a roadside snack and breather. While there, resolve to exit the nerve-splintering road first chance, even if it means altering your route; resolve further to henceforth avoid such roads.

Most drivers you'll find are considerate—only a few are barbarians. Semi-trucks are unpleasant, but their drivers are generally expert and grant you ample room when possible. However, school buses and RVs seldom budge for cyclists.

Nonmotorized hazards also merit your attention. Bridges at the bottoms of hills are often rough. Watch for and avoid sewer grates with tire-catching bars aimed your way. Ride over railroad tracks at a right angle, lest they grab your front wheel and send you sprawling. Many rural roads in the western U.S. have "cow-catchers," or "cattle guards"—series of metal bars crossing the road; dismount and cautiously *walk* across these. Finally, when riding in wetness, proceed cautiously over—or avoid—wet leaves; also, don't ride through a harm-

TOSRV photo by Greg Siple

less looking puddle, because it could be bottomless.

If you can't avoid a city, be careful riding through it. Clearly communicate your intentions to cars—use hand signals. Be alert to traffic patterns, to cars emerging from side streets, and to cars turning into your space. Most urban buses are rude fiends; treat them with the respect they don't deserve. You could ride pedestrian-absent sidewalks; better and faster are the bike lanes increasingly available in enlightened cities. If you anticipate riding through any city, write to its traffic department or visitor's bureau for a map of its cycling paths and routes.

Despite those perils, a bike tour is *not* an inherently dangerous undertaking. I have toured thousands of miles with only two minor tumbles, and I know veteran bike tourists who've experienced none. By exercising your road rights, by making yourself visible to motorists, by knowing what constitutes a hazard, and especially by choosing back roads and small towns over main roads and cities, you will complete your tour with all body parts intact, unscathed, and glowing with well-being.

How will people treat me?

While on tour, *beware of strangers!*

They'll treat you like visiting royalty, which of course you're not. They'll force-feed you nonhealthy treats like cookies, brownies, ice cream, and fried chicken. They'll delay your sacred scheduled plans with endless questions and drawling conversation. They'll sometimes weigh you down with gifts, thus sabotaging all your weight-reduction efforts. They'll destroy your solitude by taking you to meet their friends and families. They'll ruin your plans to sleep outside by insisting that you stay at their place. Finally, as if they hadn't already caused you enough turmoil, they'll send you off with well-intentioned but ultimately bum directions.

Route-side strangers are indeed the true enemies of bike tourists' rigid schedules and forward progress. Yes, while on tour, *beware of strangers*. They just might strengthen or restore your faith in humanity—that *would* be distracting!

How much will it cost?

Your main daily expenses will be for food and accommodations. The next two questions and answers discuss these, and how to cut their costs. Suffice it now to state that, with creativity, you can often sleep for free and can eat and drink for five dollars or less per day. On the other hand, if you've got plenty of money and a desire to spend it, go right ahead!

Besides eats and sleeps, miscellaneous costs that fatten your average daily expense include replacement tubes and tires, other small parts and minor repairs, bigger parts and major repairs, postage, laundry, and common replacement items like batteries and toothpaste. Other than those "major" repairs—something most touring cyclists manage to avoid—

the miscellaneous costs add less than a few dollars to your average daily expense. By only occasionally splurging on restaurant meals and motels or hostels, I keep my own average daily expense under $10. You could too.

For international touring, pre-tour research will illuminate your probable expenses. Some countries (Japan, Ireland) are more expensive, others (Mexico, India) less expensive. With foresight and creativity, you can tour cheaply in the expensive lands, too. Both food and accommodations usually cost less outside the U.S. and Canada. Miscellaneous added costs include transportation, visa costs, and the entry/exit fees charged at some borders.

If you've spent your savings on equipment and can allot only a few dollars to each day of your tour, consider these money-making possibilities: contract with a local newspaper for a series of "From the road" columns; seek sponsorship from a business or organization; market your story to newspapers along the way; sell blood plasma to plasma banks along the way.

One *BikeReport* magazine cover featured a chap on an "ongoing" tour who financed it by selling balloon "sculptures" as he went. You too have the will—now, find a way!

Where might I sleep?

When you look around, just about anywhere.

Most bike tourists zealously prefer sleeping outside to sleeping inside but occasionally do the latter. If you camp out most nights, especially if you "freelance" camp away from organized campgrounds, an indoors stopover about once a week provides a welcome chance to thoroughly clean yourself and your gear. Besides hotels and motels, your standard options include hostels and bed-and-breakfasts. Of these, hostels rank highest among touring cyclists. Motels off of beaten paths charge less than those on beaten paths. When in a college town on a summer tour, you can sometimes cheaply rent a dorm room; a fine guide to dorm rentals in North America and elsewhere is the *U.S. and Worldwide Travel Accommodations Guide*, published by Campus Travel Service (P.O. Box 5486, Fullerton, CA 92635).

Organized campgrounds are increasingly crowded and expensive. If you're concerned about security, they do offer that. They also offer showers, and you'll definitely be concerned about that! You can perhaps stay for free at state campgrounds if you arrive late and leave early, after and before the park rangers make their rounds.

For global touring, research your sleeping-space options beforehand. Hostels are more abundant in many countries than in North America, but organized campgrounds are not. Still, even lands with few campgrounds offer freelance camping opportunities. In the so-called Third World, nontourist motel and hotel rooms often cost less than campsites in the U.S., Canada, and Europe. Private homes with rooms-to-let are plentiful and inexpensive in many lands. Good general travel guidebooks discuss such budget accommodations and pinpoint sources of additional information about them.

The art of "athletic vagabonding" involves finding free sleeping-space night after night. Cultivate open eyes and an open mind, and you too can become an athletic-vagabond artist. While touring, I have slept for free in a greenhouse, in a treehouse, in a hospitable jail cell, in the empty convention room of a small casino, in a stranded, brightly colored hippie van, beneath bridges, on deserted beaches, in many small-town parks, and as an invited guest in peoples' homes everywhere I've wandered.

Wheel into a small town at dusk and request permission to sleep in their park (on the sheltered picnic table); if the town is small enough, permission will be granted. Don't sleep at roadside rests, though; they are noisy and potentially dangerous, and they often forbid camping anyhow. It's best to sleep away from the road. Exercise discretion and leave no trace. Prospects include countryside woodlands, farmers' lands (with permission), national forests, other public lands such as in the desert, beaches away from populated areas, even old rural cemeteries where your fellow lodgers will not disturb you.

When in doubt as dusk approaches, ask in a cafe or a bike shop; someone will deliver an idea if not an invitation to their home or backyard.

Wherever you sleep at night, your morning concerns include. . .

What will I eat?

Lots of stuff, massive quantities. Your appetite's size will dwarf those mountains you just huff-puffed over. The food you'll consume would satisfy entire football teams. You could eat not just a horse, but the Trojan Horse.

While satisfying your gargantuan appetite, respect nutritional requirements. They too soar on tour. Eat loads of complex-carbohydrate foods like pizza, pasta, and whole-grain anythings. Plenty of fruits, nuts, and veggies, too. Multivitamins for insurance.

Specific cycling foods? Pizza and pasta again—and again. Mexican food. Whole-grain bread with peanut butter and with fruit jam. "GORP" (good ol' raisins and peanuts) with a moderate blessing of chocolate chips; keep that, also fruit and other small snacks in your handlebar bag. Eat moderate amounts continually, your big feast at day's end.

Ideal cycling drinks? Water, water, water. Fruit juices. Water, water, water.

Foods to avoid while touring? Excessive meat and fried foods. Sugary nonfoods and drinks. Dairy products on very hot days. Caffeine and alcohol are diuretic, meaning they'll dehydrate you. But you may enjoy small amounts of tea or coffee during the day, and a cold beer or frothy milkshake at day's end.

On a tight budget? At cafes, breakfast is the least expensive meal; a bowl of oatmeal is an ideal and inexpensive engine starter. Whole-wheat bread with peanut butter and/or fruit jam nourishes yet costs little. If you take a cookstove, you can prepare nutritious, economical meals like pasta dishes and veggie stews. Roadside berries and apples beg you to sample them. Make back-room grocery-store deals for just-a-day-too-old produce and baked goods. Above all, *attend every all-you-can-eat buffet that you find*; you can eat plenty, making these a bargain.

Know before you go that a touring cyclist's staple is "See food"— when you see food, you'll want to eat it.

What about mechanical breakdowns?

By taking a mechanically sound bike, you stand a good chance of not experiencing any. I have toured on several different bikes for thousands of miles through every type of terrain without a single problem more menacing than a tire blowout. In that regard, I am not lucky but typical.

Go prepared. Preparedness requires having a competent bike mechanic thoroughly examine your bike; if the mechanic is yourself, all the better. Preparedness also requires packing all the essential repair-kit items (Chapter 1), and practicing their use beforehand.

Routine maintenance lessens the likelihood of mechanical trouble. Keep the chain and gear cogs clean and lubricated. Keep accessories tightly attached. Keep the tires fully inflated. Periodically check them, and the cables, brake pads, and wheels (for trueness of spin). Promptly replace frayed cables, worn tires, and worn brake pads. When you detect a mechanical problem, immediately check it or have it checked.

Your most likely problem, a flat tire, requires no mechanical expertise. The instructions on your patch kit will suffice for repairing simple punctures. Practice patching technique at home. Remember to always locate and remove the puncture's source. Sometimes the source comes not from the road but from your spoke-heads. This can happen when a rimstrip (the narrow rubber strip running inside your rim) breaks or gets dislocated. When fixing a flat, keep the rimstrip over your spoke-heads, and replace it (any bike shop) if it breaks. Some cyclists eliminate this potential problem by replacing rimstrips with a couple layers of electrical tape.

Books thicker than this one address bike repairs exclusively; so, instead of discussing more complicated and less likely repairs, I will recommend a few titles and then move on to other topics. For ease of mind, remember that by taking a mechanically sound bike and practicing periodic maintenance, you minimize the likelihood of breakdowns. Also know that a bike tourist is seldom far from civilization, and civilization's certain benefits always include some sort of bike shop, bike mechanic, or, at the least, a mechanical maniac-genius who, grinning, can fix *anything*.

Maintenance-repair books include both thick ones for pre-tour study and slim volumes light enough to take along. Of the former, I recommend *The Bicycle Repair Book*, by Rob Van der Plas (Bicycle Books). Of the latter, you might pack *The Bike Bag Book*, by Tom Cuthbertson and Rick Morrall (Ten Speed Press), or *Roadside Bicycle Repairs*, by Rob Van der Plas (Bicycle Books). For extremely light, cost-free take-along guidance, borrow a repair book from a library, and photocopy and pack relevant sections.

How does adverse weather affect touring cyclists?

Often and unpredictably. You cannot tour vast distances without encountering some rain, strong winds, and discomforting cold or heat. The question is not whether you'll encounter adverse weather, but whether through preparation, adaptation, and good humor you'll curtail its effect on your touring pleasure.

For rain, equip yourself well and plan to escape it. Take raingear, and perhaps fenders if you'll tour through ever-rainy regions. Because of rain-caused riding hazards—slippery surfaces, hidden potholes, and poor braking and visibility, and also because cycling in the rain is messy—scurry to the first available shelter when clouds burst. Any dry place will do, but small-town cafes do best. While there, enjoy your favorite hot drink and maybe a meal. Catch up on your journal jottings or letters home. Enjoy a long conversation with the local visionary or gossip. When an all-day rain evolves into a multi-day rain, consider allotting yourself a motel or hostel stay.

Worse than rain are troublesome winds. A strong headwind is like a seemingly endless mountain ascent, but without the satisfaction of visually charting your progress toward its end. The stronger the headwind, the harder it is to progress. Headwinds hurl dust in your eyes. They also howl in your ears, deafening you to traffic sounds. When in a headwind wear eye protection, increase your visual attention to traffic, ride low to decrease wind resistance, lower your mileage expectations, and expand your rest stops. When riding with others, take turns "drafting"—riding directly behind another cyclist. After successfully challenging a day-long headwind, reward yourself with a well-deserved extra beer or milkshake.

Nearly as troublesome as headwinds, sidewinds crowd you toward either the traffic lane or the road edge, neither one especially hospitable cycling territory. Hold steady and brace yourself for sudden side blasts. Or you can alter your course, aiming it the same direction as the wind, thus making the sidewind a temporary tailwind.

Cold is more predictable than rain and winds, and more easily avoided. Avoid it! For a nonsummer tour or a tour through colder latitudes or higher elevations, research the average temperature ranges and prepare accordingly. Dress and equip for the cold; more weight is not as bad as inadequate warmth. Especially vulnerable are your face, feet, and hands. Stay dry when riding in cold or in coolness. The gang of three—wet, wind, and coolness—can quickly cause dangerous hypothermia. Finally, remember that the cooler months have shorter days. In short, summertime is the ideal bike-touring season.

Of course, summertime tours will include occasional heat waves. Drink plenty of water, continuously—don't wait for "thirst." Apply ample sunscreen to vulnerable exposed areas like your nose and shoulders and the backs of your hands. Break frequently, under shade-giving trees and in ceiling-fan-cooled cafes. When the day burns unbearably hot, but the road is smooth, traffic nil, and evening breezes refreshing, consider night riding.

Finally, fog decreases visibility and condenses on your clothes, so sit it out awhile.

Let's briefly back-pedal to excessive heat. . . .

Surely the desert is no place for bicycling?

Yes it is. This untamed, untamable land with rugged splendor, with creatures and vegetation ingeniously adapted to its harshness, with incredibly clear air that allows you to view mountains from great distances and the nighttime heavens in unparalleled majesty, this land poetically seduces prepared bike tourists.

As with any hot-weather riding, drink continuously, before you're thirsty. When heading into a long, desolate stretch of desert, strap an extra gallon of water tight to your rack. Religiously avoid running low on water during hot desert days; if you do run low, find or devise shade near the road before you run out, and flag down a passing vehicle.

Cover your arms and legs with thin, bright, loosely fitting cotton clothing. Protect exposed skin with sunscreen. When camping in the desert night, zip your tent tightly shut to keep out snakes and scorpions while you enjoy the soulful howls of harmless coyotes. Avoid camping in a dry wash (a dry desert streambed), because a "flash flood" can attack without warning. Finally, the desert gets mighty cold during cooler-season nights, so pack adequately warm sleeping gear for desert touring then.

When warm-season touring, though, the desert shines brightest at night. For heat and wind relief, and for indescribable nighttime splendor, night-ride through the summertime desert. A night-long meteor shower might permanently bedazzle you. Beware the full desert moon, though: moonburn or even moonstroke might jumble your senses, might force you into the cacti and tumbleweed to rethink your position in the universe.

Here's a warm-season desert-touring strategy: ride at night under the moon and stars, unharried by heat and traffic. Soon after daybreak, find a motel and rent a room—for 24-plus hours; during the bright, hot day alternate among slow showers, air-conditioned naps, strolls around town, and drowsy relaxation by the pool; retire early and ride off after a midnight wake-up call, or else stay up and then sleep in late and hang around town until the next evening, *then* pedal off toward magic. Repeat this routine after each night ride.

What about mountains and big hills?

Seasoned bike tourists treasure them. They're physically demanding but mentally rewarding. The glow of accomplishment awaits at the top. If bike touring were ball playing, mountains would be the big leagues.

When riding up a mountain, shift down early and pace yourself toward the patiently waiting crest. Survey the superlative scenery as you work past and above it. Do not "push" until you must. If necessary, stand and pedal, or get off and walk—you're not modeling but getting up a mountain.

At the top of the mountain, claim it as your own; you earned it in a way that, unfortunately, few of those passing motorists could understand. Breathe deeply. Enjoy the view. Secure your load, put on a sweatshirt or jacket, check your brakes, pat yourself once more on the back, and—

Spurt down the exhilarating slope. Brake lightly and often to regulate speed, especially on curves and switchbacks. Stop at pullovers to cool your rims, recheck your brakes, and prolong the too-fleeting thrill of descent. In traffic, take the whole lane during fast descents; in or out of traffic, watch ahead for rocks, potholes, and debris.

Likewise enjoyable is cycling down-then-up hills, especially the consecutive rollercoaster-style ones. Coasting down, then halfway up, over and over, you make good time in such hills. Enjoy!

How will I keep clean?

Laundering your clothes is the simplest cleaning task. If you use coin laundries, go there wearing the least amount of clothes that is modest, and wash everything else. For global touring, note that coin laundries are rare in many countries; when you need but can't find one, try using a hotel's laundry for a small fee. One other inexpensive option is hand-laundering. Wash yesterday's outfit in campground and service-station sinks, or in clear streams and lakes (no soap there, please); strap wet clothes on top of your bags and let the sun and wind naturally dry them.

Less simple, far less when freelance camping, is keeping your hard-working body clean. Mentally and physically, you could use a shower every day, but unless you spend every night at hotels, hostels, or campgrounds, that proves difficult. I usually freelance camp on-tour, and I have found free or cheap showers/bathing the following ways: riding into a public campground, showering there, then riding merrily off; dipping into a clean lake or reservoir; stopping at gyms, spas, and YMCAs and requesting use of their showers; using community swimming pools' showers for free or maybe 50 cents, swim included; approaching a cheerful-looking motel maid early in the morning and tipping her an (often refused) two bucks for the use of the shower in any just-vacated, not-yet-cleaned room.

You might uncover other novel shower sources. Remember, too, the "Sunshower" equipment option (Chapter 1). When you haven't found any way to shower or bathe lately, carry your bath kit into a cafe or service-station restroom and scrub the high spots. Then, keep on smiling, keep on riding, and keep on looking . . .

What about dogs and other creatures?

Except in desert regions, mosquitoes will pester you the most. These loathsome insects are "international," too, so you'll not escape them short of a bike tour on the moon. In certain tropical regions they transport nasty diseases. All of which underlines Chapter 1's "Essential" ranking of insect repellent and a tent with mosquito netting.

Most dogs bark far more often and furiously than they bite. The true danger emerges when they run at you. Do *not* panic and suddenly swerve or brake—two of the worst bike accidents I've witnessed involved cyclists plunging to the pavement when startled, not bit or hit, by dogs. Carry some "Halt!" or other self-defense spray clipped onto your handlebar bag. When a dog rushes you, outsprint it if possible (most dogs don't venture far from their yards); otherwise, dismount from your bike and keep it between you and Fang. You can then spray it with mace, wave your pump at it, bark or growl back at it (my method), or even toss it a dog-bone peace offering that you just happened to have in your handlebar bag. If you and Fang make enough noise, Fang's owner should soon appear to end the standoff. Again, however you handle biker-loathing dogs, keep calm.

That's easier said than done when dealing with bears. Your ideal strategy is, of course, to *not* deal with bears! When in bear country, especially grizzly country, consider sleeping in organized campgrounds or indoors. When walking at night, shine your light and make some noise as you go—the point being to avoid surprising a bear. Don't camp near animal trails, garbage dumpsters, berry bushes, dead animals, or where you cooked your evening feast. Keep all food and food-splattered equipment (including clothing) out of your tent. Burn your food waste and place all other food items in an airtight container or garbage bag; hang this from a tree-branch so it is 10 feet above the ground and 5 feet from the trunk.

If you'll camp much in bear country, or if you're worried about wildlife generally, read a book with comprehensive advice—say, one for backpackers, who spend more time in the perilous bush than we bike tourists.

More likely than creatures to bother you . . .

Aches, pains, and itches?

You lessen the inevitable leg-muscle aches through pre-tour training, respecting your physical capacities, and stretching before and after riding. Self-massage helps soothe aches, as do over-the-counter medicated rubs. You lessen or prevent rear-end pains with pre-tour conditioning and an anatomically shaped saddle.

Lower-back aches, usually caused by an ill-fitting bike or by pushing in too-high gears, are kept minimal or nonexistent by riding a properly fitted bike and maintaining a higher cadence in lower gears. If your back complains anyhow, adjust your saddle slightly up or down.

Avid cyclists sometimes experience numb fingers. Your prevention: use handlebar padding, wear cycling gloves, and frequently change hand positions.

When all or most of these aches and pains gang up on you—a real possibility early in your tour—decrease your mileage for a few days, or take a day off.

Combining all my tours, I've endured an entire fleet of itches: athlete's foot, dandruff, sunburn, dry skin, chapped lips, and saddle sores. Remedies for all of these abound at drug stores everywhere. Still, by making every effort to keep yourself and your clothing clean and dry, and by taking proper precautions against the sun and wind, you forestall these nuisances and save the cost of remedies. If you develop saddle sores, keep the area dry and apply baby powder or cornstarch. Avoid sunburn with sunscreen. Apply lip balm to chapped lips, moisturizers to dry skin, specialized concoctions to athlete's foot and dandruff.

When planning an international tour, research the travel guidebooks for potential health hazards. Good water is hard to find in certain lands; if you'll tour through any of these, equip yourself with a water-purification method and spare change for bottled water and tummy aids. Also, if the guidebooks recommend getting vaccinations before you go, get them.

TOSRV photo by Greg Siple

How about keeping in touch with the homefront?

Besides saying "Hello!" and sharing news with the homefront, your keeping-in-touch strategy involves receiving mail drops and mailing excess stuff home.

Have mail drops sent to U.S. post offices "c/o General Delivery"; "Poste Restante" is the international term. Post offices usually hold such mail for only a limited time (10 days in the U.S.), so the sender should mark your package, "Please hold—arriving by bicycle." Have the packages sent in sufficient time for your arrival at the mail-drop town. Typical mail-drop items: a resupply of money, maps for the tour's next leg, perhaps a new book, as-needed replacement items like spare tires, of course news from home, and—this is key—home baked goodies.

Other than postcards, you might periodically mail home used maps, filled journals, rolls of film, and souvenirs from your tour. Each time you mail home such a bundle, insert a letter with news of yourself and your tour.

Keeping in touch while global touring is somewhat more complicated, but hardly impossible. Obtain detailed information from general travel guidebooks. Besides post offices, mail-drop reception options include American Express and Western Union offices. For fairly easy telephoning to the U.S. from other countries, use AT&T's "USA Direct" or MCI's "MCI Call USA" services. Both companies will send you a caller card, access number, and details about their programs. Call AT &T at **1-800-874-4000** (or, PO Box 8067, Trenton, NJ 08650-0067), MCI at **1-800-753-5225** (or, PO Box 3210, Cedar Rapids, IA 52406-9640).

Anything else?

Yes—take your time. Don't set mileage quotas you must rush to meet. In rushing, you'd miss the subtle beauties and wonders that make bike touring so rewarding. Better to take either a shorter tour or a longer time away from your normal routine.

Also, depending on both your temperament and the breaks, you might occasionally bump into on-the-road blues. If and when this happens, don't panic, and don't prematurely end your tour. Take some time off. Call home for encouragement. Scribble your woes away in your journal. Pamper yourself by finally splurging on a fine restaurant meal and hotel room. With your bike tucked safely away in that hotel, go catch a movie or two. Believe me, at some near bend in the twisting road, those nasty blues will give way to resumed exhilaration.

Finally, let your long bike tour serve as a springboard to other exceptional ventures. First-time bike tourists have become tri-athletes, arctic trekkers, mountain climbers, marathon runners, long-distance river rafters, in short, world beaters. . . .Cherish and channel the momentum and extraordinary energy that your tour will bestow upon you. ᚛

Chapter Four:
Where You Might Wander

Rise free from care before dawn and seek adventures. Let the noon find thee by other lakes, and the night overtake thee everywhere at home. There are no larger fields than these, no worthier games than may here be found.
——Thoreau

Those travellers who think that a Tahitian prays only when the eyes of the missionary are fixed on him, should have slept with us that night on the mountain-side.
——Charles Darwin

If your next question is, "Where might I tour by bike?", my immediate answer is *just about anywhere!*" The popular cycling destinations make obvious targets; less obvious yet very cyclable are the "undeveloped" world regions where, after all, self-powered transport prevails over motorized transport.

This chapter surveys very general cycling-relevant conditions, and pinpoints specific information sources for all world regions. I intend to show that you might bike-tour anywhere that attracts you, and to point you toward books and organizations that will help you thoroughly prepare yourself. The three subchapters are: the Americas (U.S.A., Canada, Mexico, Central and South America); Europe; The World—and Beyond (Africa, Asia, Australia, the Middle East, New Zealand, Russia and Ukraine, and Outer Space).

All the organizations discussed here will send you detailed information about themselves upon receiving a simple request. When writing a foreign bike club, enclose an "International Reply Coupon" (IRC—available at post offices) for their reply, and allow several weeks. Also, present them with *specific* questions (*not* "What can you tell me about bicycling in your country?").

Government tourist bureaus (Appendices 5–7) are highly recommended sources of free, sometimes cycling-specific travel information. You need not enclose return postage when writing them, but do emphasize that you'll cycle through their area. Request campground information, too.

Three other government sources are: The U.S. Government Printing Office (Washington, D.C. 20402-9325), the Consumer Information Center (Pueblo, CO 81002), and the U.S. Department of State—Bureau of Consular Affairs (Washington, D.C. 20520). All three distribute free and low-cost publications useful to U.S. citizens planning a trip abroad. Request a list of their foreign travel publications.

If you'll tour outside your own country, you have certain preparation needs. Start preparing early. Obtain a passport, and visas for countries that require them. Research into any travel advisories and health-related warnings and requirements. Discover and act upon any special equipment needs. Study your touring regions' cultural, historical, and geographical features. Shop around for, then arrange for transportation there. Good starting points for these pre-tour activities are general travel guidebooks. I'll identify those most suited to a touring cyclist's needs and aims.

A bike-touring guidebook that addresses all world regions is *Bicycle Touring International*, by Kameel Nasr (Bicycle Books, Appendix 3). Nasr, author of *The World Up Close* (reviewed in Chapter 2), has written a book useful for planning multi-country tours. He covers countries not now covered in other cycling guidebooks. For each region, he discusses climate, terrain, precautions, money matters, border crossing, and road conditions. He recommends specific routes for those countries with few decent roads. The appendices include worldwide weather tables and prevailing-wind-direction charts.

Nasr's guidebook is frequently mentioned in this chapter. Other often-mentioned sources include the Adventure Cycling Association and the Cyclists' Touring Club (Appendix 3), and Lonely Planet Publications. (Appendix 4). They all merit frequent mention because their offerings are useful for planning a wide range of bike tours.

Be it Kansas or a coastline, Alaska or Argentina, Asia or Australia or anywhere else, follow your cycling visions wherever they lead you. Souls initially more timid than yours have soared and triumphed on bike tours all over our devastatingly lovely planet. Your two-wheeled buddy is a terrific vehicle for exploring it.

The Americas

The United States

Although the U.S. has heavy motorized traffic, it also has a tremendous variety of cyclable roads, a huge assortment of campgrounds, and an amazing diversity of terrains. Some of its most spectacular cycling roads are: Highway #1 on the Pacific Coast, Blue Ridge Parkway and Skyline Drive in the Appalachians, Going-to-the-Sun Road in the northern Rockies, and Avenue of the Giants in the California Redwoods. The most spectacular regions are the Southwest, the Northwest, the Sierra Nevada, the Rockies, the Appalachians, the West Coast north of Southern California, and New England at the time of brilliant autumn hues.

Experienced cyclists touring ocean-to-ocean often ride west to east because prevailing winds blow that direction. If you're planning such a tour, ride whichever direction you'd like, but don't follow the too-often repeated advice to "Skip the 'boring' Midwest." Its people are earthy, its summers lush, its backroads plentiful.

Design a tour based on your own interests. Take a national-park tour, a covered-bridge tour, a Civil War battle-site tour, a hot-springs tour, a ghost-town tour, or a museum tour. Although I urge you to route your tour around any place so big and bustling as Chicago, if you are there, visit the fascinating **Bicycle Museum of America.**

For maps and information, the **Adventure Cycling Association (ACA,** Appendix 3) is your best U.S. source. ACA's stated mission is "to inspire individuals to use the bicycle for adventure, exploration, and discovery." They mapped the Trans-America Route from Astoria, Oregon, to Yorktown, Virginia. This meandering route annually attracts thousands of cross-country cyclists. Other ACA routes traverse the Mississippi Valley, the West Coast, the East Coast, the country via both the northern and southern states, and the national parks in the majestic Northwest. A "Great Lakes Trail" is under development. ACA routes use quiet, scenic backroads. With precise turn-by-turn directions, and useful notes about route-side facilities and area climate and terrain, their map-sleeve-sized maps are ideal for bike touring.

ACA (formerly "Bikecentennial") also sells a variety of cycling books. Many of these include maps and describe routes; between them, they cover every U.S. region and chunks of Canada, Mexico, Europe, Africa, Asia, Australia, and New Zealand. Although ACA sells maps and books to anyone, its 30,000-plus members get them at a slight discount. Other membership ($22 annually) benefits include a subscription to the entertaining, tour-oriented *BikeReport* magazine, and a copy of the annually updated *Cyclist's Yellow Pages*, an outstanding resource directory. To

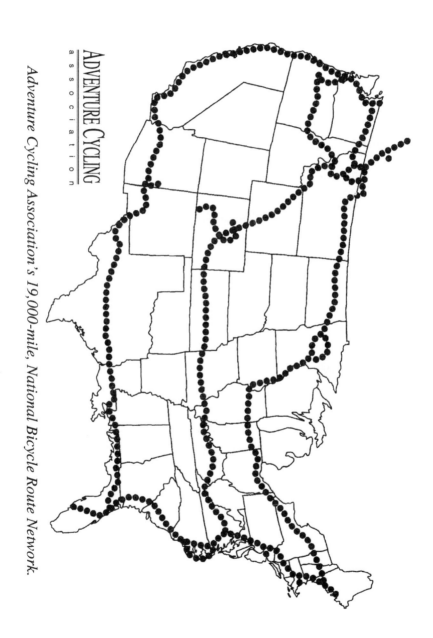

Adventure Cycling Association's 19,000-mile, National Bicycle Route Network.

inquire about membership or their offerings, you need only ink, paper, and a stamped envelope.

The **League of American Wheelmen** (**LAW**) has supported cyclists' rights in the U.S. for over a century. LAW is not a touring club like ACA, but members receive publications relevant to tour planning and gain access to "Ride Information Directors" in all 50 states. LAW members also have access to the club's Hospitality Homes program—a directory of other LAW members scattered about the land who'd welcome you as an overnight guest when on tour. For information, call **1-800-288-BIKE**, or write (190 W. Ostend St., Suite 120, Baltimore, MD 21230-3755).

An independent Hospitality Homes program that requires not that you pay a membership fee, but that you agree to be listed as a touring cyclists' host, is **The Touring Cyclists' Hospitality Directory**. Operated by bike tourist John Mosley, this program lists about 500 hospitable homes. Foreign tourists coming to the U.S. can obtain the directory without obligation. For information about this big-hearted operation, send a stamped, self-addressed envelope (7303 Enfield Ave., Reseda, CA 91335).

Again, the Adventure Cycling Association sells cycling guidebooks for every region of the country. One book describing a cross-country route is *Bicycling Across America*, by Robert Winning (Wilderness Press, Appendix 3). Winning thoroughly details a transcontinental route from L.A. to Washington D.C., via the southern states. Included are rough maps, route descriptions, elevation gain/loss information, photographs, and grinning commentary. This is a good guide for rebels who prefer southern to northern.

The best single guide to bike paths and routes throughout the U.S. is—believe it or not—a *campground* guide. Woodall's *Plan-It—Pack-It—Go* describes bike routes both short and long in most states. As mentioned in Chapter 2, it also lists campgrounds throughout North America and includes other useful information.

All state tourist bureaus (Appendix 5) will send you free road maps, campground guides, and general traveler's literature. Upon request, some also send excellent cycling-specific material, including bike-route maps; as I write, the best free cycling information comes from the tourist bureaus of Arkansas, Delaware, Maine, Maryland, North Carolina, North Dakota, Pennsylvania, Texas, Utah, and Wisconsin. This can change, though, so request cycling information when contacting *any* tourist bureau.

No travel guidebook can possibly cover the entire country in other than a skimpy manner, but *Let's Go: USA* makes a good starting point while you await the tourist-bureau material.

For personal descriptions of bike touring in the U.S., read one of the narratives recommended in Chapter 2.

Canada

Canada has 60,000 kilometers of coastline, zillions of fresh-water rivers and lakes, spectacular western mountains, and free-roaming wildlife galore. It is officially bilingual (English and French). About 40% of Canadians cycle, so bike shops and spare parts are widely available.

Although Canada is relatively expensive for standard travelers, cycling travelers can greatly lessen expenses by camping and/or staying at youth hostels. Canada's 60-some hostels are spread most thickly along the southeast coastal region, the St. Lawrence Seaway, and Alberta's Rocky Mountains—fine cycling areas all. There are more than 2,000 official campgrounds; scenery-wise, the superlative ones are in the national and provincial parks. Freelance camping opportunities exist throughout the wide-open spaces.

Ignoring for now Canada's infamous biting flies and monstrous mosquitoes, the best bike-touring months are mid-May through September.

The coast-to-coast Trans-Canada Highway (#1) has generally wide shoulders but is mighty busy near cities. You can find mellower paved roads throughout southern Canada. Farther north, roads become fewer, less crowded, and less often paved. The Icefields Parkway in western Alberta ranks as a world-class cycling route; youth hostels and campgrounds abound in this Eden of montane splendor.

Canada's clearinghouse for books, maps, and other cycling information is the **Canadian Cycling Association** (**CCA**, Appendix 3). They sell bike-touring route books for every section of the country. For localized information, they can refer you to regional bike-club affiliates. Write CCA for details and a publications catalog.

ACA also sells cycling guidebooks to several regions of Canada. A single guide to the entire country is the *Canadian Cycling Association's Complete Guide to Bicycle Touring in Canada*, by Elliot Katz. Available from CCA, it includes general information, equipment suggestions, and specific route descriptions with maps.

The provincial tourist bureaus are outstanding sources of free cycling-relevant information. Besides the usual road maps, campground guides, and general traveler's literature that they all send, the following ones include detailed cycling advice and/or route maps: Alberta, British Columbia, Manitoba, New Brunswick, Newfoundland, and Prince Edward Island.

If, after delving into the tourist bureaus' information, you desire yet more, dig into a Let's Go or Lonely Planet guidebook to Canada. For a charming personal report, read *Miles From Nowhere*.

Mexico

Ah, Mexico! Road and traffic conditions can drive you *loco*. You must beware of drinking any but bottled water. Women must also beware of assertive, unsolicited male attention.

But Mexico moves not at a rat-race's but a bike tourist's pace. Necessities cost little. Paved, low-traffic roads run from town to town. Rain is scarce nearly everywhere, year-round warmth abundant nearly everywhere. The varied natural settings aim for the heart. If not bike shops, at least skillful, inventive mechanics reside in every town. The border is easily crossed, the food zesty, the citizenry warm and spirited. Shall we go?

Sí, sí, but not before some pre-tour research. Any good travel guidebook to Mexico will whisper warnings and precautions about the water, the *policia,* male "machismo," and the possibility of catching some diseases; still, only the water needs your constant vigilance. The guidebooks will also discuss language (natives appreciate any efforts), money matters (great news!), and gotta-go attractions away from the crowded common ones. They will likely warn you about Mexico City's filthy air—when on a bike, heed that warning!

Let's Go: Mexico, The Mexico and Central American Handbook, and Lonely Planet's "Travel Survival Kit" for Mexico all give good general advice and specific recommendations. *The People's Guide to Mexico* by Carl Franz (John Muir Publications) gives few specific recommendations, but it does give a wealth of thoughtful advice. You can find these at travel stores (including the mail-order ones in Appendix 4), or at many libraries—not a bad idea, since they're all too bulky to take.

The national tourist bureau (Appendix 5) will send you a road map, though the AAA stocks better ones.

If you'll cycle extensively in sunny Mexico, your best resource is *Bicycling Mexico,* by Eric Elman and Erika Weisbroth (Hunter Publishing). The personable authors' research involved cycling throughout Mexico, on every kind of road, through every kind of terrain. They give thoughtful tips on cycling and traveling in Mexico generally, cycling in each of the country's regions, and specific routes both long and short. This is a thorough guide, with interesting anecdotes reflecting the Mexico bike-touring experience. Available from the Adventure Cycling Association, and at some libraries.

Two other books, *Bicycle Touring International,* and *Latin America by Bike* (reviewed in the next section), each have a section on Mexico; however, *Bicycling Mexico* is your best single guide.

Central and South America

When planning a tour to this exotic region, pre-tour research is vital. You'll learn that prices are low nearly everywhere, that winters are mild in all but high-elevation areas, that most countries have a distinct rainy season, that vaccination and inoculation recommendations abound, that politeness and friendliness are expected and are returned by most natives, and that spectacular unspoiled natural beauty awaits you there.

Road conditions vary more than a two-year-old's moods, but you can find decent roads in every country except, perhaps, Bolivia. The Pan Am Highway—a.k.a. "The Gringo Trail"—is cyclable throughout, hence popular among cyclists touring the West Coast. The countries with the best roads and other conditions conducive to pleasurable bike-touring are: Argentina, Belize, Brazil, Chile, Costa Rica, Ecuador, Peru, Uruguay, and Venezuela.

Argentina, Brazil, Chile, Columbia, Ecuador, Peru, and Uruguay have scattered youth hostels; inexpensive nonhostel accommodations are plentiful.

By far your most comprehensive general-information source is the **South American Explorers Club (SAEC)**. A nonprofit club with offices in New York, Peru, and Ecuador, SAEC stocks an Amazon-sized collection of maps, guidebooks, and descriptive literature on all of Central and South America. That includes "Trip Reports" written by adventuring club members and loads of bicycling information.

You need not be a member to order from SAEC's catalog of map and book offerings, including several bike-touring books. Substantial membership ($30 annually) privileges include free Trip Reports, reduced prices on the catalog offerings, a subscription to the club's quarterly journal, consultation with staff members when tour planning, and access to the club's South American clubhouses. Whether or not you join, if you're planning a South American excursion, send for their publications catalog (U.S. Headquarters, 126 Indian Creek Road, Ithaca, NY 14850).

Inside SAEC's catalog is every type of general travel guidebook. The best single title is *The South American Handbook*—a.k.a "The Bible" for traveling there. (Central American countries get covered in the *Mexico and Central American Handbook*.) The second-best general guidebooks are Lonely Planet's "On a Shoestring" guides, one for Central, one for South America. *Adventure Travel in Latin America,* by Scott Graham (Wilderness Press), is also helpful.

The only complete cycling guide to this region is a good one: *Latin America by Bike* by Walter Sienko (The Mountaineers) covers all countries. General travel information, cycling and equipment tips, map sources and road conditions, intelligent discussions of cultural aspects, descriptions and rough maps of recommended routes in 13 countries—Sienko gives everything except his favorite guacamole recipe! Unlike the general travel guidebooks, this book is light and small enough to pack. Perhaps you should borrow one of the guidebooks from a library, copy notes from it into your journal, and obtain Sienko's book to take along. It is available from the Adventure Cycling Association and the SAEC.

Other sources include *Bicycle Touring International*, the Cyclists' Touring Club (CTC), and a small book titled *Latin America on a Bicycle*, by J.P. Panet (Passport Press). The first of these has a fairly detailed section on South America that includes some specific routing advice. CTC is an outstanding club discussed in the subchapter on Europe; it offers members "Information Sheets" on cycling in various areas, including most Central and South American countries. Panet's book is far less useful than the other two bike-touring titles, but it does have some routing information for the Dominican Republic, Venezuela, Argentina, Chile, Costa Rica, and Guatemala—at last glance, it was available from the SAEC.

Two narratives recommended in Chapter 2, *Two Wheels and a Taxi* and *The World Up Close*, personalize the South American bike-touring experience.

Europe

Preparing for a European bike tour involves more than preparing for a North American one, less than for tours elsewhere. Options abound for transportation there. English is widely spoken and understood. Numerous backroads are paved and well maintained. Prices and facilities are generally similar to those in the U.S. and Canada. Health and travel warnings are few, border crossings usually simple. North American travelers of every stripe and style are common. One difference, happily to your advantage: youth hostels are plentiful throughout Europe.

Europe attracts hordes of bike tourists and teems with native cyclists. You're seldom far from a bike shop or bike mechanic. Bike lanes and paths run hither and thither. Although road conditions are generally superb and most countries have extensive networks of cycling-ideal backroads, these countries are the best for cycling: Belgium, Denmark, France, Germany, Great Britain, Greece, Holland, Ireland, Turkey, and Austria and Switzerland if you can handle the mountains (you can!).

Of course, customs and cultures vary from region to region, likewise climate and terrain. Your preparation needs will alter accordingly. If touring through the mountains or through northern or Mediterranean countries other than in summer, pack additional clothing and sufficient camping gear. If you've got wheels other than 700mm, pack a spare tire. Finally, you'll need a passport, and visas for some countries—apply early.

For visiting lots of Europe on limited time, consider getting a Eurail Pass; with one, you could pedal through favored areas and train-travel elsewhere. The inter-nation Eurail train system is fairly inexpensive, is cyclist-accommodating, and goes nearly everywhere (except Great Britain). Many travel agents and mail-order travel stores stock Eurail literature and sell the various types of Eurail tickets. All general travel guidebooks to Europe have sections on Eurail usage.

As for any multi-country touring, your preparation includes research. A fine starting point is a letter to the **Cyclists' Touring Club (CTC,**

Appendix 3). This nonprofit cyclists' organization—the oldest in the world—diligently secures and defends cyclists' road rights. They have 40,000 members worldwide and 200 affiliated clubs. Their Touring Department supplies comprehensive, updated "Information Sheets" on cycling in some 60 countries and detailed routes within and between those countries. This service is free to members. Countries covered include all European ones (Great Britain most extensively), the U.S., Canada, Mexico, Australia, New Zealand, and countries in Africa, Asia, the Middle East, and Central and South America.

CTC compiles and updates the Information Sheets from reports of members who have cycled the regions. The "sheets" vary in length (a half-page to nearly a dozen), but all provide useful information. Typical information includes terrain, climate, road conditions, route suggestions, general travel tips, and relevant resources such as maps, books, and area cycling clubs.

If touring far from home, consider joining CTC. Besides requested Information Sheets, members receive the club's various informative pamphlets, their bimonthly magazine *Cycle Touring and Campaigning*, and price breaks on cycling accessories, clothing, and maps. CTC also sells a wide range of bike-touring books. Enclose an IRC when writing them for details.

Your number-one source of *free* road maps, traveler's literature, and (sometimes) cycling-specific tips and maps, are the European tourist bureaus (Appendix 6). The ones that'll mail you, upon request, extensive cycling information are: Denmark, Germany, Great Britain, Holland, Hungary, Ireland, Sweden, and Switzerland. Also, many European towns and cities have local tourist-bureau offices offering localized cycling tips and maps. When in Europe, use them.

For regional small-scale maps that show biker-friendly backroads, write to CTC, Maps By Mail (Appendix 4), or Michelin (Appendix 4; yes, they're the tire company, founded over a century ago on the strength of their innovative

TOSRV photo by Greg Siple

bicycle tires!). Michelin's small-scale maps are clear and detailed. They also publish "Green Guides" to Europe, these among the most suitable general travel guidebooks to the continent. Also suitable are *Let's Go: Europe*, Lonely Planet guidebooks, and Rick Steves's *Europe Through the Backdoor*. All recent editions of guidebooks to Europe have added increasing amounts of cycling coverage, a trend that will no doubt continue.

CTC, the Adventure Cycling Association, and the Backcountry Bookstore stock a multitude of cycling guidebooks to Europe, both the entire continent and several individual countries (France, Great Britain, Holland, Ireland, Italy). These vary in usefulness, but all have specific route recommendations. With Europe's fine system of roads, you do not downright *need* an extensive cycling guidebook—especially if you take advantage of the tourist-bureau offerings and obtain small-scale maps and/or CTC's Information Sheets. Regarding cycling guidebooks, the Europe section in *Bicycle Touring International* is adequate; because of its extensive advice on cycling elsewhere, I recommend it.

Among the narratives discussed in Chapter 2, you'll find interesting accounts of cycling through Europe in *Miles From Nowhere, The Long Ride, The World Up Close*, and *One Time Around*.

As long as you're pedaling through Europe, you might keep on pedaling, might just wheel through. . .

The World—and Beyond

More about that "Beyond" business later; for now, the world is plenty far enough! Might you pedal all around the world? *Yes!!!* In many ways, the world-less-traveled will accommodate you and your bike tour. Outside the industrialized Western World, life moves more slowly, traffic at about the speed of you on your bike; walking and bicycling are principal means of personal transportation. In heavily touristed areas, natives learn to resent travelers from afar, but in the world's sleepy villages and backwater hamlets, visiting travelers are usually welcomed and valued—it's like, "You rode that contraption that far just to visit *us*?" Read *Miles From Nowhere, The World Up Close, Off the Map*, or *The Long Ride* for glimpses of the priceless encounters available in out-of-way places.

The farther you pedal from home, the more you'll need to research beforehand. Heed travel advisories and health precautions. Learn something of the cultures' customs, practices, and languages. Know in advance the cost of food and overnight accommodations. Scour the libraries and bookstores for travel guidebooks, and for literature inspired by the countries you'll wheel through. If you can find books about cycling there, read them.

In the upcoming sections, we'll scan general relevant conditions and review specific sources of specialized information. In this order, we'll peek at Africa, Asia, Australia, the Middle East, New Zealand, and Russia and Ukraine. Then we'll pack our bikes and go to Togo or Nepal.

Africa

As I write, Americans and Europeans cycle in Africa—and they will continue cycling there, perhaps in pursuit of what Kameel Nasr terms "One of life's most rewarding experiences." Cycling in Africa, that is.

Car traffic is negligible outside of cities and generally courteous where it does exist. Overnight accommodations cost less than an American fast-food lunch. Since many Africans cycle, basic bicycle parts are widely available. Hospitality you can expect. The countries most suited to cycling, primarily meaning those with the best road systems, are: Algeria, Ivory Coast, Kenya, Libya, Malawi, Morocco, Nigeria, Senegal, Togo, Tunisia, Uganda, Zambia, and Zimbabwe.

As visa and entry requirements and health warnings vary from country to country, as Africa is a vast, diverse continent with every type of terrain, over 50 nations, and hundreds of languages, I'll generalize little more and instead urge you to research ahead of time, starting with. . .

Bicycling in Africa, by David Mozer (International Bicycle Fund, 4887-R Columbia Dr. S., Seattle, WA 98108) qualifies as "required reading" if you'll tour in Africa. It is for general adventure travelers as well as bike tourists, but from a bike-tourist's perspective. The slim book has brief country-by-country discussions of bike-touring conditions in Algeria, Benin, Burkina Faso, Cameroon, Ghana, Ivory Coast, Kenya, Malawi, Mali, Niger, Nigeria, Senegal, Tanzania, Togo, Tunisia, and Zimbabwe.

Other main topic areas include cultural awareness, body maintenance, health and wellness, preparing for bicycle travel in Africa, motorized transport options, accommodations, personal security, and border crossings. The detailed appendices are useful, too. Available from its publisher, the Adventure Cycling Association, and some libraries.

International Bicycle Fund also sells "supplements" to *Bicycling in Africa* that cover smaller areas in far greater detail. Titles include: Kenya; Zimbabwe/Botswana; Ghana/Togo/Benin; Malawi/Tanzania/Uganda; Tunisia/Algeria; Mali/Burkina Faso/Niger; Senegal/Gambia; and Cameroon. Each supplement includes information on routes, maps, and rural accommodations. Prices range from $5 to $10. Write IBF for further details and current ordering information.

Bicycle Touring International is another valuable source of cycling-specific tips about Africa. It has country-by-country discussions and a number of route recommendations. Use it in addition to—not in place of—*Bicycling in Africa*.

Cyclists' Touring Club members can access the following Information Sheets: Algeria, Tunisia, Libya, Morocco, The Sahara, Egypt and Sudan, Gambia, Ghana, West Africa, Black Africa, Kenya, Zambia, Zimbabwe, Malawi, Namibia, South Africa, and Seychelles.

Michelin is your best source of African road maps. Lonely Planet publishes "Travel Survival Kits" for individual regions and a big, budget-minded "On a Shoestring" guide to the entire continent. The Sierra Club (Appendix 3) publishes several adventure-travel guides to east and north Africa. Probably the best general travel guidebook for bike-touring purposes, though, is *Through Africa: The Overlander's Guide*, by Bob Swain and Paul Snyder (Bradt Publications, 41 Nortoft Road, Chalfont St. Peter, Bucks SL9 OLA, England). Written for adventurers, it includes cycling guidance.

African tourist bureaus that offer useful travel literature appear in Appendix 7.

Finally, *Miles From Nowhere, One Time Around*, and—extensively—*The World Up Close* and *The Long Ride* contain telling chapters set in Africa.

Asia

Certainly, you'll have better success finding the Eastern World than did Christopher Columbus and crew; once there and cycling about, equally certain is the likelihood of finding or re-finding yourself. Also certain is that you'll encounter hordes of native cyclists, generally very low prices (exception: Japan), plenty of decent paved roads, and a delicious diversity of landscapes. The Asian countries most suited to bike touring are: China, India, Japan, Malaysia, Pakistan, Nepal, South Korea, Sri Lanka, and Thailand. All Asian countries, though, are cyclable.

There are scattered youth hostels in Hong Kong, India, Malaysia, Pakistan, and Thailand; Japan has over 400, making it possible to tour cheaply there, too. Inexpensive nonhostel accommodations are abundant throughout the Asian mainland.

Enjoy some armchair travels with contemporary books about Asian lands and people. Delve into good travel guidebooks. Lonely Planet guides are recommended; between their "Travel Survival Kits" and "On a Shoestring" guides, they blanket the continent. Instead of packing these hefty volumes, extract copious mental and written notes.

Cyclists' Touring Club members have access to Information Sheets on China, Hong Kong, India, Indonesia, Japan, Malaysia, Pakistan, Philippines, Singapore, South Korea, Sri Lanka, and Thailand.

Bicycle Touring International gives general advice and tips for the whole continent, and specific cycling conditions in all countries—some routing suggestions, too.

Bike-touring information is otherwise scarce for most other Asian countries, but not for Japan. *Bicycling Japan*, by Suzanne Lee (Zievard Press, PO Box 1018, Davis, CA 95617) is a take-along-sized book with expert advice and usable information on traveling by bike in Japan. Try its publisher or your library. A newer guidebook, *Cycling Japan*, is edited by Bryan Harrell, founder and publisher of Japan's English-language cycling newsletter, *Oikaze*. I've not read the book, but am told it includes general advice, maps, route recommendations, and anecdotes and reflections from *Oikaze* contributors. (For information: Kodansha America, 114 Fifth Ave., New York, NY 10011.) The quarterly, nonprofit newsletter supplies personal tour narratives, cycling tips, and free personal ads. For details and a sample issue, send a self-addressed envelope with an IRC (Oikaze, 2-14-4-306, Tomigaya-Cho, Shibuya-Ku, Tokyo 151 Japan).

Asian tourist bureaus that will send you free information appear in Appendix 7. For the smaller countries, the tourist-bureau maps should suffice; otherwise, inquire of Appendix 4's mail-order travel stores.

The Adventure Cycling Association's and Backcountry Bookstore's catalogs list several personal-experience books I've not read about bike tours through Asia. Four I have read, and reviewed in Chapter 2: *Miles From Nowhere* describes cycling adventures in India, Nepal, South Korea, Malaysia, and Thailand; *The World Up Close* in India, Nepal, and China; *One Time Around* in India, Thailand, and Malaysia; *The Long Ride* in India, Nepal, Malaysia, Singapore, and several dreamy Indonesian islands.

Note that none of the cyclist-authors bypassed colorful India. Note, too, that they all wisely avoided cycling through Asia during the monsoons.

Australia

Similar in size to the continental U.S. but with opposite seasons and a sparser population, Australia lures many adventurers and many bike tourists. The language is English, the water drinkable, and the terrain variable. Cyclable roads are plentiful, freelance camping opportunities abundant, and inexpensive accommodations available—Australia has over a hundred youth hostels. A network of rural bike trails is under development.

Start by writing the accommodating tourist bureau (Appendix 7). Tell them what you're planning, and they'll mail you free cycling information, including routing recommendations. Most general travel guidebook publishers print a volume on Australia; given the chance, read Lonely Planet's. Many travel stores stock Australian road maps.

Bicycle Touring International's brief segment on Australia imparts a few helpful facts and tips, though hardly enough to merit its price solely for planning a tour here. The Cyclists' Touring Club stocks an Information Sheet for Australia worth checking out if you're a club member.

For extensive guidance, read *Bicycle Touring in Australia*, by Leigh Hemmings (The Mountaineers). It's thoughtfully written and beautifully photographed by its author, an enthusiastic bike tourist. After an entertaining introduction and some practical matters, she thoroughly describes eight routes through different sections of the country, rough maps included. The book's appendix lists bike shops throughout Australia. It is bulky, though, so I recommend borrowing it from a library and copying desired information. If you've an itch to own it, the Adventure Cycling Association and the Backcountry Bookstore sell it.

The Long Ride elaborates Lloyd Sumner's splendid time cycling and goofing off in Australia, and you'd have a splendid time reading it—especially if you're headed there.

The Middle East

This volatile region is for extremely adventurous cyclists only. The widespread anti-Western sentiment is reportedly subsiding, but political turbulence will likely continue. Read current travel-guidebooks and pay attention to current news reports. Study Middle East cultures and customs, and respect them while there. Both men and women will need to replace cycling shorts with cycling pants. On the positive side, road systems are generally adequate, and, like everywhere else, the hospitality of everyday people might surprise you.

Lonely Planet publishes "Travel Survival Kits" for Iran, Israel, Jordan & Syria, and Yemen. *Let's Go: Israel & Egypt* is useful, too, and it includes information on Jordan and the West Bank. If you're near a university, you might seek out students from the Middle East, take them to lunch, ask a few key questions, and listen as they talk.

For maps, inquire at travel stores.

The Cyclists' Touring Club has Information Sheets for Syria, Jordan, Israel, Iran, and the Arabian Peninsula. The only cycling guidebook that covers this region, *Bicycle Touring International*, encourages you to tour here in its chapter on the Middle East. It addresses general cycling conditions in Syria, Lebanon, Israel, Jordan, Iraq, Iran, and the Arabian Peninsula, and suggests some specific routes.

A chapter in *The World Up Close* describes author Nasr's bike travels and encounters in Israel.

New Zealand

An English-speaking nation, New Zealand has moderate prices, safe drinking water, and no major or widespread health risks. Add decent roads with light traffic (other than meandering herds of sheep and cattle).

Add a rugged, rural, sparsely populated cycling-scape. Add mild temperatures (though very windy). Add farmlands, geysers, hot springs, fjords, forests, glaciers, snow-capped mountains, and wave-whipped shorelines. Add hundreds of hostels and campgrounds, small motels and hotels, country pubs and private homes with rooms-to-let; add to those a multitude of freelance camping opportunities. Add a bike shop in every town. It all adds up to a bike tourist's Nirvana—New Zealand.

Start with the tourist bureau (Appendix 7) for a free map and other travel literature. Then leaf through any good travel guidebook. Recommended: *Adventuring in New Zealand*, by Margaret Jefferies (Sierra Club Books)—it includes cycling tips. If you're a member of the Cyclists' Touring Club, request their New Zealand Information Sheet.

The Canterbury Cyclist's Association (P.O. Box 2547, Christchurch, New Zealand, Attn: Mr. Alex Ferguson) extends complimentary advice to visiting cyclists. They also sell cycling (and kayaking) guides to the islands. These are published by SeaLand Publications (12 Dunn Street, Christchurch 2, New Zealand). When writing the club, ask specific questions, and enclose a couple IRCs for their reply.

Cycle Touring in New Zealand, by Bruce Ringer (The Mountaineers), exhaustively covers both the North and South islands—the climate, money matters, accommodations, and road conditions. It describes recommended routes, too, 14 connected ones. You can get it from its publisher, from the Adventure Cycling Association, or from Backcountry Bookstore—unless you'd like to save both money and touring weight, in which case you should look for it at a library.

The World Up Close, One Time Around, The Long Ride, and *Miles From Nowhere* each has a chapter set in New Zealand. A clue: the chapter in *Miles* is titled, "World's Friendliest Folks."

Russia and Ukraine

The travel situation in the former Soviet Union has changed since I started writing this, and it will undoubtedly change again by the time that you read this. As I write, travel in Russia is still restricted, but the restraints should slowly unravel. Travel in the Ukraine is—right now—unrestricted. On the negative side, both cultures remain sexist, both countries become mighty cold outside of summertime, and both have few campgrounds.

On the positive side, cyclists have found it possible to tour there and have found some decent roads; if you too have an urge to cycle there, of course you must go, the sooner the better.

Start by writing Russia's Intourist office (Appendix 7); clearly state your aims and needs. You'll also want to read the most recently updated travel guidebook you can find. Try either Lonely Planet's or else *The*

Baltics & Russia Through The Backdoor (Europe Through The Backdoor, 109 Fourth Avenue N., PO Box C-2009, Edmonds, WA 98020)—whichever is most recent.

St. Petersburg now has a youth hostel—easily the least expensive tourists' lodgings in town. You can contact their Los Angeles office for hostel information as well as trip-planning advice and an update on travel conditions in Russia. (RYHT, 409 N. Pacific Coast Hwy., Bldg. 106, Suite 390, Redondo Beach, CA 90277; Tel: 310-379-4316).

If you're a member of the Adventure Cycling Association or the Cyclists' Touring Club, you have access to their updated Cyclists' Yellow Pages and Information Sheets, respectively. In time, both will likely include new sources and information on bike touring in this region.

Off The Map is a terrific read that will familiarize you with the conditions you'll face. And, no—I don't think either *War and Peace* or *The Brothers Karamazov* justifies its weight, cycling-wise.

And Beyond

Bolt your armchair to the floor and belt yourself in: Starting with *Bicycling Through Space and Time*, continuing with *The Ultimate Bike Path* and *The 22nd Gear*, and leading I'm-not- sure-where, is a series of far-flung sci-fi cycling novels by Mike Sirota (Ace Books). These make transcontinental and global tours seem like comparatively short jaunts. Cycling in alien worlds, in the earth's distant past, in the afterlife, *everywhere!*

Is this a trend? Will we soon see cycling guidebooks to other dimensions, Adventure Cycling Association maps of Mars, Cyclists' Touring Club Information Sheets to the past and the future?

These novels also raise this pleasant question: Wouldn't gravity-free bike touring be *wonderful*? ᨁ

The Appendices

It is thrifty to prepare today for the wants of tomorrow.
——Aesop

*We hug the earth,—how rarely we mount! Methinks we might elevate
ourselves a little more. We might climb a tree, at least.*
——Thoreau

Appendix 1:
Equipment Checklists

(Review Chapter 1 for discussion of these.)

· · · · · · · · · · · Attachments · · · · · · · · · · · ·

Essential
Lighting system
Lock
Pump
Rear rack
Water bottles and cages

Optional
Bell/horn
Computer/odometer

Optional (cont'd.)
Fenders
"Flickstand"
Front rack
Handlebar pads
Mirror
Safety flag
Seat pad
Toe clips
Tube protection system

· · · · · · · · · · · · · · Bags · · · · · · · · · · · · · · ·

Essential
Handlebar bag
Kit bags
Misc. bags and baggies
Rear saddlebags

Optional
Backpack, small
Front saddlebags
Seat bag
Stuff sack

· · · · · · · · · · · Camping gear · · · · · · · · · · · ·

Essential
Cord/rope
Flashlight and batteries
Insect repellent
Knife
Sleeping bag
Sleeping pad
Tent

Optional
Camper's pillow
Candle/candle lantern
Collapsible water container

Optional (cont'd.)
Cookstove & cookware
Cooking oil
Fire-starter chips
Foil
Groundcloth
Pillowcase
Pocket saw
Pot scrubbers
Sheet bag (essential for hostel stays)
Tent-repair kit
Waterproof matches/lighter

· · · · · · · · · · · · · Kit—Bath · · · · · · · · · · · · · ·

Essential
Comb or brush
Contact lens, case, & solutions
   (if worn)
Cotton swabs

Essential (cont'd.)
Deodorant
Feminine hygiene items
Mirror
Nail clippers

· · · · · · · · · · Kit—Bath (cont'd.) · · · · · · · · · ·

Essential (cont'd.)
Shampoo (conditioner)
Soap
Toilet paper
Tooth brush & paste/powder
Washcloth

Optional
Cosmetics
Shaver(s)
Skin moisturizers
Sunshower
Towelettes

· · · · · · · · · · · · · Kit—Chow · · · · · · · · · · · · ·

Essential
Can opener
Eating utensils
Spice mix/salt & pepper
Vitamins

Optional
Water-purification method
(essential for touring some countries)

· · · · · · · · · · · Kit—First Aid · · · · · · · · · · · · ·

Essential
Antiseptic
Baby powder/cornstarch
Bandages, various sizes
Cloth medical tape
Pain relievers
Prescription medicine
Sterile gauze pads

Optional
Antibiotics
Dental emergency kit
First-aid booklet
Needle
Snake-bite kit
Special medications
Tweezers

· · · · · · · · · · · · · Kit—Repair · · · · · · · · · · · · ·

Essential
Allen wrenches
Bolts and nuts, spare
Brake cable, spare
Cable ties
Derailleur cable, spare
Electrical tape
Handcleaner and rag
Lubricant
Patch kit
Pliers
Spoke tool
Strip of tire
Tire levers
Wrench, multi-fit

Essential (cont'd.)
Screwdrivers
Spokes, spare

Optional
Air-pressure gauge
Ball bearings, spare
Bottom-bracket tools
Chain tool and chain-link master
Extra-hand tool
Freewheel removal tool
Grease
Inner tube, spare
Pedal wrench
Tire, spare

· · · · · · · · · · · · · Clothing · · · · · · · · · · · · · ·

Essential
Raingear
Shirts, several
Shoes, one pair

Essential (cont'd.)
Shorts, two pair
Socks, several pair
Sweats

· · · · · · · · · · · Clothing (cont'd.) · · · · · · · · · · ·

Essential (cont'd.)

Sunglasses
Underwear/liners

Optional

Booties
Bra(s)
Gloves, cycling
Headband/bandanna
Helmet
Money belt
Safety goggles
Semiformal outfit

Cool-weather options

Arm warmers
Leg tights
Face mask/balaclava
Gloves, full-fingered
Jacket/parka
Sweatshirt(s)
Thermal underwear

· · · · · · · · · · · Odds & Ends · · · · · · · · · · · ·

Essential

Chapstick/lip balm
Emergency information card
Identification card
Journal/paper and pencil
Maps
Sunscreen
Towel

Optional

Alarm clock
Book
Breath freshener
Camera and film
Cards—access/credit/membership

Optional (cont'd.)

Compass
Ear plugs
Field glasses
Fishing gear
"Halt!"/mace spray
Ham radio, hand-sized
Harmonica
Magnifying glass
Music headset
Penlight, disposable
Safety pins, twist ties, rubber bands
Sink plug
Water-flavoring mix

· · · · · · · · Global Tourist's Miscellanea · · · · · · · ·

Bank certificate
Birth certificate
Cards, international
ID backup
Important addresses

Passport w/visa stamps
Phrase booklets/lists
Prescription information
Transportation tickets
Vaccination certificates

Appendix 2:
Selected Equipment Suppliers

(Includes cycling and camping; free catalogs upon request)

Bike Nashbar: 4111 Simon Road, Youngstown, OH 44512; **1-800-627-4227**

Branford Bike: 1074 Main St., Branford, CT 06405; **1-800-272-6367**

Campmor: 810 Route 17 N., PO Box 997-G, Paramus, NJ 07652; **1-800-526-4784**

Off The Beaten Track: 1504 E. Michigan Ave., Lansing, MI 48912 (bike touring equipment)

Performance Bicycle: PO Box 2741, Chapel Hill, NC 27514; **1-800-727-2433**

Recreational Equipment, Inc. (REI): 1700 45th St. E., Sumner, WA 98352-0001; **1-800-426-4840**

Terry Precision Bicycles for Women: 1704 Wayneport Rd., Macedon, NY 14502; **1-800-289-8379** (informative catalog especially for women cyclists)

Trek Bicycle Corporation: 801 W. Madison, PO Box 183, Waterloo, WI 53594 (No mail-order sales, but they will send an informative catalog.)

Appendix 3
Selected Book Sources

(Includes both publishers and distributors—request catalogs)

Adventure Cycling Association: PO Box 8308, Missoula, MT 59807

The Adventurous Traveler Bookstore: Box 577, Hinesburg, VT 05461

Backcountry Bookstore: PO Box 191, Snohomish, WA 98291-0191 (Extraordinary selection of cycling, outdoors, and travel books!)

Bicycle Books: PO Box 2038, Mill Valley, CA 94942

Canadian Cycling Association: 1600 Prom. James Naismith Dr., Gloucester, Ontario K1B 5N4 Canada

Cyclists' Touring Club: Cotterell House, 69 Meadrow, Godalming Surrey GU7 3HS England

The Globe Pequot Press: PO Box 833, Old Saybrook, CT 06475-0833

The Mountaineers Books: 1011 S.W. Klickitat Way, Suite 107, Seattle, WA 98134

Rodale Press: 33 E. Minor St., Emmaus, PA 18098

Sierra Club Books: 100 Bush St., San Francisco, CA 94104

Wilderness Press: 2440 Bancroft Way, Berkeley, CA 94704-1676

Women In The Wilderness: 566 Ottawa Ave., St. Paul, MN 55107 (Good source of books by and about women adventurers)

Appendix 4:
Selected Mail Order Travel Stores

(Maps, guidebooks, and traveler's literature. Some of them will hunt down requested maps or guidebooks that they do not normally stock.)

Book Passage, 51 Tamal Vista Blvd., Corte Madera, CA 94925; **1-800-321-9785**

The Complete Traveller Bookstore, 199 Madison Ave., New York, NY 10016; 1-212-685-9007 ($2.00 for this catalog)

Forsyth Travel Library: PO Box 2975, Shawnee Mission, KS 66201; **1-800-367-7984**

Lonely Planet Publications: 155 Filbert St., Suite 251, Oakland, CA 94607-2538; **1-800-275-8555** (Publishers of travel guidebooks recommended throughout Chapter 4)

Maps By Mail: PO Box 52, San Leandro, CA 94577; 1-510-483-8911 (Small-scale maps of Europe and North Africa)

Michelin Travel Publications: PO Box 3305, Spartanburg, SC 29304-3305; **1-800-223-0987** or **1-800-423-0485**

Rand McNally Map & Travel Stores: Not a mail-order business, but they operate a chain of good travel stores. Call **1-800-333-0136** for their outlet closest to you, or for questions, special requests.

The Savvy Traveller: 50 E. Washington St., Chicago, IL 60602; 1-312-263-2100

Appendix 5:
Tourist Bureaus—
The Americas

(In this order: U.S. states, Canadian provinces, Mexico, selected Central and South American countries. Watch for toll-free numbers in **bold** print. *denotes some cycling information included; **denotes substantial cycling information, such as routing guidance and/or bike maps. Always make clear that you'll cycle through, also that you'll camp, if you will.)

U.S.A.

Alabama Bureau of Tourism and Travel: PO Box 4309, Montgomery, AL 36103-4309; **1-800-ALABAMA**

Alaska Division of Tourism: PO Box 110801, Juneau, AK 99811

Arizona Office of Tourism: 1100 W. Washington St., Phoenix, AZ 85007

****Arkansas** Department of Parks and Tourism: 1 Capitol Mall, Little Rock, AR 72201; **1-800-NATURAL**

California Office of Tourism: 801 K St., Suite 1600, Sacramento, CA 95814; **1-800-862-2543**

Colorado Tourism Board: PO Box 38700, Denver, CO 80238; 1-800-433-2656

Connecticut Tourism Development: 865 Brook St., Rocky Hill, CT 06067; **1-800-CT-BOUND**

****Delaware** Tourism Office: 99 Kings Hwy., PO Box 1401, Dover, DE 19903; **1-800-441-8846**

Florida Division of Tourism: 126 Van Buren St., Tallahassee, FL 32399-2000

Georgia Tourist Division: PO Box 1776, Atlanta, GA 30301; **1-800-VISIT-GA**

Hawaii Visitors Bureau: PO Box 2359, Honolulu, HI 96804

***Idaho** Travel Council: 700 W. State St., State House Mall, Boise, ID 83720; **1-800-635-7820**

***Illinois** Bureau of Tourism: 310 S. Michigan Ave., #108, Chicago, IL 60604; **1-800-223-0121**

Indiana Tourism Division: 1 North Capitol, Suite 700, Indianapolis, IN 46204; **1-800-289-6646**

***Iowa** Bureau of Tourism: 200 E. Grand Ave., Des Moines, IA 50309; **1-800-345-4692**

Kansas Travel and Tourism, Dept. of Commerce: 700 S.W. Harrison St., Suite 1300, Topeka, KS 66603; **1-800-2KANSAS**

***Kentucky** Travel Development: 500 Metro St., Capitol Plaza Tower, 22nd Floor, Frankfort, KY 40601; **1-800-225-8747**

Louisiana Office of Tourism: PO Box 94921, Baton Rouge, LA 70804 **1-800-33-GUMBO**

****Maine** Publicity Bureau: PO Box 2300, Hallowell, ME 04347-2300; **1-800-533-9595**

****Maryland** Office of Tourism: 217 E. Redwood St., Baltimore, MD 21202. **For Bicycle Info: 1-800-252-8776**

Massachusetts Office of Travel and Tourism: 100 Cambridge St., 13th Floor, Boston, MA 02202; **1-800-447-6277**

Michigan Travel Bureau: PO Box 30226, Lansing, MI 48909; **1-800-543-2937**

*Minnesota Office of Tourism: 375 Jackson St., Room 250, St. Paul, MN 55101; **1-800-657-3700**

Mississippi Division of Tourism: PO Box 22825, Jackson, MS 39205

Missouri Division of Tourism: PO Box 1055, Jefferson City, MO 65102; **1-800-877-1234**

Travel **Montana**: 1424 Ninth Ave., Helena, MT 59620; **1-800-541-1447**

*Nebraska Tourism Office: PO Box 98913, Lincoln, NE 68509; **1-800-228-4307**

Nevada Commission on Tourism: Capitol Complex, Carson City, NV 89710; **1-800-638-2328**

New Hampshire Office of Vacation Travel: PO Box 856, Concord, NH 03302-0856

New Jersey Division of Travel and Tourism: 20 W. State St, CN 826, Trenton, NJ 08625-0826; **1-800-JERSEY-7**

New Mexico Tourism and Travel Division, 1100 St. Frances Dr., Santa Fe, NM 87503; **1-800-545-2040**

New York Division of Tourism: 1 Commerce Plaza, Albany, NY 12245; **1-800-225-5697**

North Carolina Travel and Tourism: 430 North Salisbury St., Raleigh, NC 27603; **1-800-847-4862

North Dakota Tourism Promotion: Liberty Memorial Building, Bismarck, ND 58505; **1-800-437-2077 (From Canada: 1-800-537-8879)

*Ohio Division of Tourism: PO Box 1001, Columbus, OH 43266; **1-800-BUCKEYE**

Oklahoma Tourism and Recreation Department: PO Box 60789, Oklahoma City, OK 73146; **1-800-652-6552**

*Oregon Tourism Division: 775 Summer St. N.E., Salem, OR 97310; **1-800-547-7842**

Pennsylvania Bureau of Travel: 453 Forum Building, Harrisburg, PA 17120; **1-800-847-4872

Rhode Island Tourism Division: 7 Jackson Walkway, Providence, RI 02903; **1-800-556-2484**

South Carolina Department of Parks, Recreation & Tourism: Division of Travel & Tourism, PO Box 71, Columbia, SC 29202; **1-800-872-3505**

*South Dakota Department of Tourism: Capitol Lake Plaza, 711 Wells Ave., Pierre, SD 57501; **1-800-952-3625**

Tennessee Department of Tourism: PO Box 23170, Nashville, TN 37202-3170; **1-800-VISIT-TN**

**Texas Travel & Information Division: PO Box 5064, Austin, TX 78763-5064

**Utah Travel Council: Council Hall, 300 N. State, Salt Lake City, UT 84114

*Vermont Travel Division: 134 State St., Montpelier, VT 05602

Virginia Tourism Division: James Center, 1021 E. Cary St., Richmond, VA 23219; **1-800-VISITVA**

Washington Tourism Division, 101 General Administration Bldg., Olympia, WA 98504-0613; **1-800-544-1800**

West Virginia Travel and Tourism: Department of Commerce, State Capitol, Charleston, WV 25305; **1-800-CALL-WVA**

Wisconsin Division of Tourism Development: 123 W. Washington Ave., Madison, WI 53707; **1-800-432-8747

Wyoming Division of Tourism: Frank Norris, Jr. Travel Center, Cheyenne, WY 82002; **1-800-225-5996**

Canada

Alberta Tourism: Box 2500, Edmonton, Alberta T5J 2Z4 Canada; **1-800-222-6501 in province; 1-800-661-8888

Tourism **British Columbia: Parliament Buildings, Victoria, British Columbia V8V 1X4 Canada

Travel **Manitoba: 7th Floor, 155 Carlton St., Winnipeg, Manitoba R3C 3H8 Canada; **1-800-665-0040, ext. 20**

Tourism **New Brunswick: PO Box 12345, Fredericton, New Brunswick E3B 5C3 Canada; **1-800-442-4442 in province; 1-800-561-0123**

Newfoundland and **Labrador** Dept. of Development and Tourism, PO Box 8730, St. Johns, NF A1B 4K2 Canada; **1-800-563-6353**

Northwest Territories—**"Travel Arctic"**: Box 1320, Yellowknife, NWT XIA 2L9 Canada; **1-800-661-0788**

Nova Scotia Department of Tourism: PO Box 456, Halifax, Nova Scotia B3J 2R5 Canada

*Ontario** Travel: Queens Park, Toronto, Ontario M7A 2R9 Canada; **1-800-668-2746**

Prince Edward Island Dept. of Tourism and Parks: Visitor Services, PO Box 940, Charlottetown, Prince Edward Island C1A 7M5 Canada

Tourisme Quebec: Case Postale 20,000, Quebec (Quebec) G1K 7X2 Canada; 1-800-363-7777

*Tourism **Saskatchewan**: 1919 Saskatchewan Dr., Regina, Saskatchewan S4P 3V7 Canada; **1-800-667-7538 in province; 1-800-667-7191**

*Tourism **Yukon**: PO Box 2703, Whitehorse, Yukon Y1A 2C6 Canada

Mexico

Mexican Tourism Council: 10100 Santa Monica Blvd., #224, Los Angeles, CA 90067, or 405 Park Ave., #1401, New York, NY 10022

Central and South America

Argentina Government Tourist Information: 12 W. 56th St., New York, NY 10019

Belize Tourist Bureau: 15 Penn Plaza, 415 7th Ave., New York, NY 10001

Chile: LanChile Airlines: 9700 S. Dixie Highway, 11th Floor, Miami, FL 33156

Columbian Government Tourist Office: 10 E. 46th St., New York, NY 10017

Peru: Peruvian Tourism Promotion Board: 444 Brickell Ave., #M-135, Miami, FL 33131

Appendix 6:
Tourist Bureaus—Europe

(Again, *denotes some cycling info., ** denotes substantial cycling info. such as routing guidance and/or bike maps.)

Austrian National Tourist Office: 500 Fifth Ave., 20th Floor, New York, NY 10110

Belgian National Tourist Office: 780 Third Ave., Suite 1501, New York, NY 10017

Bulgarian National Tourist Office: Balkan Holidays, 41 E. 42nd St., #508, New York, NY 10017

***Cyprus** Tourist Office: 13 E. 40th St., New York, NY 10016

Czechoslovak Travel Bureau and Tourist Office (CEDOK): 10 E. 40th St., New York, NY 10016

****Denmark**: See **Scandinavian Tourist Boards**

***Finland**: See **Scandinavian Tourist Boards**

French Government Tourist Office: 610 Fifth Ave., New York, NY 10020

****German** National Tourist Office: 122 E. 42nd St., 52nd Floor, New York, NY 10168

****Great Britain**: British Tourist Authority: 551 Fifth Ave., New York, NY 10176

Greek National Tourist Organization: Olympic Tower, 645 Fifth Ave., New York, NY 10022

Holland: see **Netherlands**

****Hungarian** Travel Bureau (IBUSZ): 1 Parker Plaza, Suite 1104, Fort Lee, NJ 07024

Iceland Tourist Board: 655 Third Ave., 19th Floor, New York, NY 10017

****Irish** Tourist Board: 345 Park Ave., 17th Floor, New York, NY 10154; **1-800-223-6470**

Italian Government Travel Office (ENIT): 630 Fifth Ave., Suite 1565, New York, NY 10111

***Luxembourg** Tourist Information Office: 17 Beekman Place, New York, NY 10022

Monaco Tourist and Convention Bureau: 845 Third Ave., New York, NY 10022; **1-800-753-9696**

Netherlands Board of Tourism: 225 N. Michigan Ave., Suite 326, Chicago, IL 60601

***Northern Ireland** Tourist Board, 551 Fifth Ave., Suite 701, New York, NY 10176-0799; **1-800-326-0036**

***Norway**: See **Scandinavian Tourist Boards**

Portuguese National Tourist Office: 590 Fifth Ave., 4th Floor, New York, NY 10036; **1-800-767-8842**

Romanian National Tourist Office: 342 Madison Ave., Suite 210, New York, NY 10173

****Scandinavian** Tourist Boards (For Denmark, Finland, Norway, Sweden): 655 Third Ave., New York, NY 10017-5617

Spanish National Tourist Office: 8383 Wilshire Blvd., Suite 960, Beverly Hills, CA 90211

****Sweden**: See **Scandinavian Tourist Boards**

****Swiss** National Tourist Office: 608 Fifth Ave., New York, NY 10020

Turkish Tourist Office: 1717 Massachusetts Ave. N.W., Suite 306, Washington, DC 20036

Appendix 7:
Tourist Bureaus—
Worldwide

(Generally, only those countries that realize/pursue substantial tourism income from the U.S. maintain a tourist bureau here. This list will likely expand with time; if you do not find a listing here for a country you'll tour through, check the most recent travel guidebook for that region; at the least, you can write that land's embassy.)

Africa

Egyptian Tourist Authority: 645 N. Michigan Ave., Chicago, IL 60611
Kenya Tourist Office: 424 Madison Ave., New York, NY 10017
Moroccan National Tourist Office: 20 E. 46th St., New York, NY 10017
Nigeria Tourist: 828 Second Ave., New York, NY 10017
Tunisia Embassy, Tourist Section: 1515 Massachusetts Ave. N.W., Washington, DC 20005
Togo Information Service: 1706 R St. N.W., Washington, DC 20009
Uganda Tourism: 336 E. 45th St., New York, NY 10017-3489
Zambia National Tourist Office: 237 E. 52nd St., New York, NY 10022
Zimbabwe Tourist Office: 1270 Avenue of the Americas, #412, New York, NY 10020

Asia

China National Tourist Office: 333 W. Broadway, Suite 201, Glendale, CA 91204
Hong Kong Tourist Association: 590 Fifth Ave., 5th Floor, New York, NY 10036-4706
Government of **India** Tourist Office: Suite 15, North Mezzanine, 30 Rockefeller Plaza, New York, NY 10112
Indonesian Tourist Promotion Office: 5 E. 68th St., New York, NY 10021
Japan National Tourist Organization: 401 N. Michigan Ave., Suite 770, Chicago, IL 60611
The **Korea** Society: 950 Third Ave., 8th Floor, New York, NY 10022 (Not a tourist bureau, but a source of travel information)
Malaysia Tourism Promotion Board: 818 W. Seventh St., Los Angeles, CA 90017
Pakistan Tourism: 12 E. 65th St., New York, NY 10021
Singapore Tourist Promotion Board: 333 N. Michigan Ave., Suite 818, Chicago, IL 60601
Sri Lanka Tourist: 2148 Wyoming Ave. N.W., Washington, DC 20008
Taiwan Visitors Association: 1 World Trade Center, #7953, New York, NY 10048
Thailand Tourism Authority: 5 World Trade Center, Suite 3443, New York, NY 10048

Australia

**Australian Tourist Commission: 489 Fifth Ave., 31st Floor, New York, NY 10017

The Middle East

*Israel Government Tourist Office: 5 S. Wabash Ave., Chicago, IL 60603
Jordan Information Bureau: 2319 Wyoming Ave. N.W., Washington, DC 20008
Saudi Arabia Tourism: 866 U.N. Plaza, #480, New York, NY 10017

New Zealand

*New Zealand Tourism Board: 501 Santa Monica Blvd., Suite 300, Santa Monica, CA 90401; **1-800-388-5494**

Russia

Intourist Travel Information: 610 Fifth Ave., #603, New York, NY 10020

Appendix 8:
In Case the Spokes Broke—
A Tear & Take Sheet

If/when a spoke or two (or three—spokes snap like dominoes drop, one after the other) breaks, you'll hear, feel, or sense it. Stop immediately; one fallen spoke can quickly create trouble for your entire bike.

Pull out your repair kit. You'll need those essential-ranked spare spokes and spoke wrench—which you practiced using at home, right? If your spoke(s) broke on the freewheel side of your rear wheel, you'll also need either a bike shop or that optional-ranked freewheel removal tool that you conservatively packed, also a wrench.

Front-wheel spokes break far less often—less tension, less weight. If the broken spoke fortunately is a front one, you simply bend it over double, unscrew it with your spoke tool, and yank out a willing spare to screw into the broken one's place. Maintain the spoke design's over/under status quo. Tighten the new spoke about as tight as neighboring spokes, and spin the wheel to check trueness.

If the spoke(s) broke on the freewheel side of your rear wheel, you need to remove that freewheel, which would (naturally!) rather not budge.

Remove the rear wheel from the bike and the quick-release lever from the wheel. Your freewheel remover fits snugly inside the freewheel grooves. Tightly holding the wheel vertically, use your wrench to exert strong downward (counterclockwise) pressure on the remover. That freewheel will be— #!¿ ¶x—mighty tight. If you can't budge it, find a farmer or mechanic and borrow a longer-handled wrench, also possibly a vise in which to clamp the wheel. (Don't seek out a bike shop yet; you're almost done.)

As salty sweat streams into your sensitive eyes, 'tis time to gently chide yourself: "Should've got a bike with at least 40 rear-wheel spokes, thick spokes at that; should've also kept my weight low, my wheels trued—if not by myself, by a bike mechanic; should change my ways regarding these!"

Finally. . . **the freewheel breaks free**. At this time, you gleefully unscrew it by hand, and replace the broken spoke just as you do a front-wheel one. Hand-tighten the freewheel back on (the wheel's movement on the waiting road will tighten it #!¿ ¶x tight again). Replace the quick-release lever on the wheel, the wheel on the bike, yourself on the bike-seat, and the bike on the road.

Now, really: did you have to rip a page out of a perfectly good book for a maneuver as simple as that?!

Index